RAND NATIONAL DEFENSE RESEARCH INSTITUTE

T0146139

Improving U.S. Military Accession Medical Screening Systems

Maria C. Lytell, Kimberly Curry Hall, Nelson Lim

Prepared for the Office of the Secretary of Defense

For more information on this publication, visit www.rand.org/t/RR2780

Library of Congress Cataloging-in-Publication Data is available for this publication.

ISBN: 978-1-9774-0366-7

Published by the RAND Corporation, Santa Monica, Calif.

© Copyright 2019 RAND Corporation

RAND® is a registered trademark.

Support RAND

Make a tax-deductible charitable contribution at
www.rand.org/giving/contribute

www.rand.org

Preface

To ensure that the military is using effective and efficient accession medical screening processes for enlisted and officer applicants, the Office of the Deputy Assistant Secretary of Defense for Military Personnel Policy, Accession Policy asked RAND Corporation researchers to evaluate current accession medical screening systems, review past efforts to reform the two existing systems, identify potential options for future reforms, and develop a plan for a pilot program that potentially combines key features of the two systems and integrates input from key stakeholders.

This research was conducted within the Forces and Resources Policy Center of the RAND National Defense Research Institute (NDRI), a federally funded research and development center sponsored by the Office of the Secretary of Defense, the Joint Staff, the Unified Combatant Commands, the Navy, the Marine Corps, the defense agencies, and the defense Intelligence Community.

For more information on the RAND Forces and Resources Policy Center, see www.rand.org/nsrd/ndri/centers/frp or contact the director (contact information is provided on the webpage).

Contents

Figures and Tables

Summary

Every year, the U.S. military evaluates hundreds of thousands of applicants to determine their eligibility to serve, including their medical fitness. Two Department of Defense (DoD) organizations conduct medical screenings of the applicants during the accession process using somewhat different methods and different medical providers for two different groups: enlisted and officer applicants. The quality of these screenings is important because they have a direct impact on armed forces recruiting and readiness. The services want to retain all dedicated applicants who are medically fit and qualified to serve and to avoid costs associated with those unfit to serve (e.g., training losses from medical separations).

To ensure that the military is using effective and efficient accession medical screening processing systems, the Office of the Under Secretary of Defense for Personnel and Readiness/Military Personnel Policy, Accession Policy (OUSD/P&R/MPP [AP]) asked RAND's National Defense Research Institute (NDRI) to examine the current accession medical screening processing systems, review past efforts to reform the two systems, and determine whether there is a more effective and efficient way to conduct these medical screenings, potentially by combining the two system. NDRI conducted interviews and focus groups with stakeholders, reviewed the existing research, and examined prior DoD efforts to reform the process. Based on this information, NDRI identified three main courses of action (COAs) to reform the business models used for accession medical screening and the potential feasibility of implementing each COA.

Two Separate Systems for Accession Medical Screening Processes

Two DoD organizations—the U.S. Military Entrance Processing Command (USMEPCOM) and the Department of Defense Medical Examination Review Board (DoDMERB)—are responsible for the medical screening of applicants.

USMEPCOM oversees the medical screening (and other entrance requirements) of enlisted applicants at 65 Military Entrance Processing Stations (MEPS) in the United States as well as a small number of officer applicants (e.g., health care professionals). Near the end of fiscal year (FY) 2018, more than 396 MEPS medical personnel had administered about 305,000 medical examinations (USMEPCOM, undated). In addition to government personnel, USMEPCOM uses contract medical providers who work on-site and are monitored and trained by DoD.

DoDMERB oversees the medical screening of officer applicants to U.S. military service academies, Reserve Officers' Training Corps (ROTC) scholarship programs, and Uniformed Services University of the Health Sciences (USUHS), among others. Contract medical providers at over 400 sites around the United States screen about 30,000 officer applicants annually, according to information provided by a DoD-MERB representative in 2019. DoDMERB contracts with Concorde Inc. to provide medical services and execute key steps in the process.

Figures S.1 and S.2 provide an overview of how the two screening processes work. Figure S.1 depicts the USMEPCOM process for screening applicants (which follows a prescreening process based on applicant responses to questions on prescreening forms). The examination process begins with applicants checking in at the medical control desk, receiving a brief on the medical screening process, and then completing additional screening forms. Once forms are complete, applicants undergo exams (e.g., sight, hearing) with medical technicians, provide biological samples (e.g., urine) for testing (e.g., for presence of drugs), and are examined and interviewed by medical providers, many of whom are physicians. Once the examination is complete, providers evaluate the applicants against Department of Defense Instruction (DoDI) 6130.03, *Medical Standards for Appointment, Enlistment, or*

Figure S.1
USMEPCOM In-Person Medical Screening Process for Enlisted Recruits

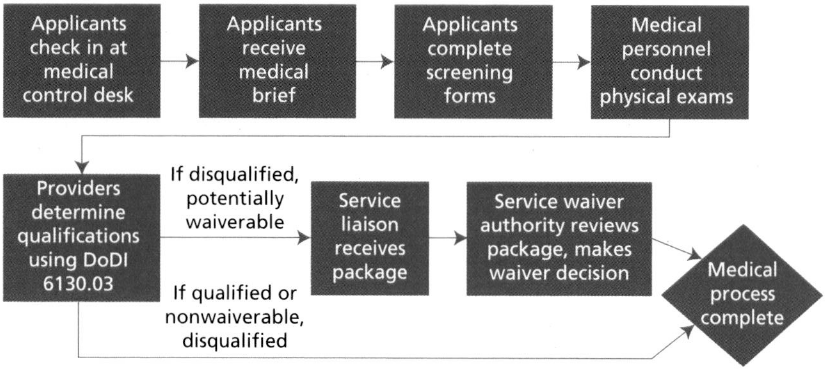

SOURCE: USMEPCOM Regulations 40-1 (2018) and 601-23 (2017).

Induction into the Military Services. Qualification determinations are made by government providers (i.e., the MEPS chief medical officer [CMO], assistant CMO [ACMO]) or contract health providers with a level of MEPS certification to enable them to profile applicants.

If the applicant is qualified, the medical screening is complete and the applicant can continue the process to screen for admission to the service. If a qualified MEPS medical provider determines that an applicant is disqualified for nonwaiverable reasons, the medical screening process is complete, and the applicant is rejected. If the MEPS medical provider determines the applicant has a medical disqualification that the service might waive, the MEPS medical section sends the applicant's medical package to that service's liaison, who is responsible for sending the package to the appropriate Service Medical Waiver Review Authority (SMWRA) for review. For applicants seeking waivers, the medical screening process ends when the SMWRA decides whether to grant or deny the waiver.

Figure S.2 depicts the DoDMERB medical screening process for applicants from service academies and ROTCs. The process typically starts with accession sources notifying DoDMERB to provide medical screening for a set of applicants. DoDMERB mails letters to the applicants with instructions on logging in to the scheduling system of the

Figure S.2
DoDMERB Medical Screening Process for Academy and Reserve Officer Training Corps Applicants

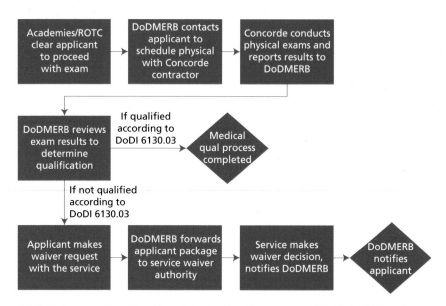

SOURCE: Personnel and Readiness Information Management (P&R IM, 2015) and discussions with DoDMERB subject matter experts (SMEs).
NOTE: An exception to the second step of the process exists for ROTC applicants who are based on college campuses. These applicants can go directly into the Concorde system for scheduling their examinations without waiting for letters from DoDMERB.

medical screening contractor, Concorde Inc. Applicants schedule initial examinations (medical, vision, hearing) at Concorde locations near them. Concorde's contracted medical providers conduct the examinations and send results to DoDMERB. DoDMERB's medical staff reviews the packages and makes the qualification determination using the same DoDI that MEPS medical providers use (DoDI 6130.03). If the applicant is deemed medically qualified, the medical screening process is complete. If the applicant is determined to be medically disqualified, the applicant can request a waiver review from the service. DoDMERB sends the applicant's package to the appropriate service medical waiver authority, which conducts the review. DoDMERB notifies the applicant of the waiver review decision, thus completing the process.

Issues with Current Systems

To explore the feasibility of combining the two accession medical systems, we conducted interviews and focus groups with key stakeholders to understand their concerns and perspectives. We first spoke with representatives from USMEPCOM and DoDMERB to learn about potential issues they might see with a combined system and to ensure we acknowledged or addressed their concerns. We also conducted interviews and focus groups with stakeholders whom we considered to be "customers" of the USMEPCOM and DoDMERB systems due to their experience with the processes and related outcomes of these systems. USMEPCOM customers included enlisted recruiters (in focus groups) and representatives from U.S. Army Recruiting Command and U.S. Army Medical Department (from interviews). DoDMERB customers included admissions representatives from service academies and representatives from ROTCs. The interviews and focus groups revealed that each system has perceived strengths and weaknesses, as outlined below. It is worth noting that despite potential concerns from stakeholders about combining the current systems, DoDMERB and USMEPCOM currently work collaboratively to execute their organizational missions effectively.

Perceptions of DoDMERB's Process

USMEPCOM representatives questioned the quality of exams offered by DoDMERB's contracted medical providers. Although both organizations use contracted medical providers, USMEPCOM contractors are trained by USMEPCOM personnel in "accession medicine," they work on-site under the chief medical officer's purview, and they are part of the process for deciding whether an applicant is qualified, disqualified, or waiverable.[1] DoDMERB neither directly monitors the training provided to Concorde contractors nor supervises them at centralized sites; however, DoDMERB contractors are not part of the direct decisionmaking process.

---

[1] According to USMEPCOM (2016, p. 22), accession medicine, defined as "evaluating the suitability of the moral, physical, and mental condition of prospective applicants for entry into military service," is a unique capability of USMEPCOM medical departments.

USMEPCOM stakeholders also perceived that hometown doctors, if contracted to perform medical screening, might advocate for applicants who may not be qualified and might fail to provide a purely objective medical assessment. USMEPCOM stakeholders also noted that medical providers untrained in accession medicine might be less likely to detect undisclosed health issues because they are not familiar with that approach.

Perceptions of USMEPCOM's Process

Alternatively, DoDMERB stakeholders found the USMEPCOM process to be inconvenient, time-consuming for both applicants and the recruiters helping with screenings and paperwork, and a potential threat to recruiting. USMEPCOM has just 65 screening sites, while DoDMERB contracts with hundreds of medical providers across the country. As a result, some recruits without transportation may lack access to USMEPCOM sites, and others will have the expense of travel, if not provided by recruiters, and time away from work or school. USMEPCOM also lacks a system to make appointments online. It is important to note, however, that although DoDMERB has an online appointment system, some DoDMERB stakeholders voiced frustration with incompatible information technology (IT) systems that cause duplication of effort.

DoDMERB stakeholders also had concerns about exposing officer applicants to elements of enlisted military culture at MEPS, including their "cattle calls" and "hurry up and wait" procedures, which officer applicants might find off-putting or unfamiliar. For example, if an applicant were deciding between the U.S. Air Force Academy or an elite civilian university, these factors could drive the applicant toward the civilian university. In addition, recruiters complained of a lack of consistency across the 65 MEPS sites, perceiving some as more efficient or more likely to qualify applicants than others. They also mentioned that recruits with seemingly the same medical issues required different types of documentation and received different waiver determinations, which makes it difficult for recruiters to prepare applicants for the screening process.

Recruiters also perceived a lack of transparency and accountability in the MEPS process. They considered the USMEPCOM medical screening process a black box in which MEPS contractors do not answer questions from applicants and recruiters have little visibility into the person's status, so an applicant's questions go unanswered.

System Advantages and Disadvantages

Based on our review of the two systems and findings from USMEPCOM and DoDMERB stakeholders, we outline the key advantages and disadvantages of each system relative to one another in Table S.1.

Attempts at Reforming Accession Medical Processing

DoD has sought to improve how it processes applicants for medical fitness in both the past and present. Ongoing efforts primarily involve working groups of key stakeholders (including DoDMERB and USMEPCOM representatives) to standardize and streamline efforts, as well as modernize data standards and management systems. However,

Table S.1
Relative Advantages and Disadvantages of the DoDMERB and USMEPCOM Systems

	DoDMERB	USMEPCOM
Advantages	• Greater number of locations decreases travel time and cost requirements • Online scheduling convenience • Less potential for wait time at exams • Civilian medical exam environment is familiar to applicants	• Exams conducted by medical providers trained in and regularly exposed to accession medicine • Serves as a one-stop shop for numerous pre-accession functions for enlisted applicants • System designed to process large number of applicants
Disadvantages	• Private physicians have less exposure to accession medicine than at MEPS • Serves only medical mission; applicants must go elsewhere for other pre-accession requirements • System currently designed for limited number of applicants	• Fewer locations result in increased travel time and cost • Lack of online scheduling convenience • Greater potential for wait time at exam • Military medical exam environment is unfamiliar to some applicants and may not be well received

ongoing efforts are not aimed at the fundamental business models of either system. In the mid-2000s, DoD leaders did commission efforts in two states to examine how a hybrid system allowing applicants to choose either DoDMERB or MEPS for screening would affect costs and applicants' "customer" experiences, among other outcomes. These efforts "failed to launch," and the basic question of whether a hybrid medical screening system could provide greater efficiencies and higher-quality outcomes than two separate systems remained unanswered.

The individual services have also pursued ways to modify medical screening approaches for their own uses. An attempt by the Army National Guard (ARNG) in 2008 to allow applicants to receive physicals from medical providers of their own choosing was discontinued in 2011 due to quality concerns. In the early-mid 2000s, the Army Medical Department (AMEDD) attempted to provide medical professionals accessing into the Army the option of MEPS, military treatment facilities (MTFs), or DoDMERB exam locations but ran into challenges for their unique population of medical professionals. A Marine Corps effort begun in 2010 to allow applicants for Officer Candidate Course (OCC) and Platoon Leaders Class (PLC) to be screened at either USMEPCOM or DoDMERB locations continues to operate, having processed over 4,100 people between 2010 and 2014. We had intended to evaluate the Marine Corps program, but found the data to be insufficient, among other limitations. However, we provide the data elements we requested as a way to help DoD track the data if it were to evaluate the program.

Courses of Action to Reform Accession Medical Screening Processing Systems

We identified three main COAs that DoD could undertake to reform the accession medical screening processing systems.

1. Use a high outsource model that sends all applicants to off-site health care providers for medical screening (akin to the DoDMERB system).

2. Use a low outsource model that sends all applicants to MEPS for medical screening.
3. Develop a hybrid model in which applicants can go to either DoDMERB or MEPS.

COAs 1 and 3 can have variations. For example, COA 1 could involve (a) all applicants going through DoDMERB or (b) USMEPCOM contracting with off-site providers for the applicant population that USMEPCOM currently serves. COA 3 could range from a DoDMERB-heavy to MEPS-heavy approach in terms of applicant flows.

We used three criteria to assess the potential impact of each COA on DoDMERB and USMEPCOM: (1) organization, (2) capacity, and (3) information-sharing. We find that each COA can have major impacts on both organizations' accession medical screening systems but that the impacts will vary by COA. For DoDMERB, COA 2 has the largest impact overall as it would effectively remove DoDMERB from the business of accession medical screening. For USMEPCOM, COA 1a (DoDMERB conducts all medical screening) has the greatest potential impact. Outside these two extreme scenarios, the hybrid COA 3 has the greatest unknown impact in terms of how applicant flow would affect system capacity and potentially the greatest impact on information-sharing, as both DoDMERB and MEPCOM would need to communicate with all accession sources and each other as applicants can flow through either system.

Although COA 3 could have major impacts, it may be the least risky of the three COAs for DoD to adopt. Unlike COAs 1 and 2, COA 3 is not designed to significantly disrupt the organizational structures and staffing of MEPS or DoDMERB. (However, we acknowledge that maintaining the infrastructure and staffing levels of both organizations has the potential to be less efficient than focusing resources on just one organization, as with COAs 1 and 2.) COA 3 is also the only COA that would allow population cross-flows (i.e., some enlisted applicants would go through the DoDMERB system while some officer applicants would go through MEPS). Finally, COA 3 has a template in the United States Marine Corps (USMC) OCC/PLC program that DoD could consider expanding to other accession sources. However, even an expansion of the USMC OCC/PLC program would not address fundamental questions about the effectiveness and efficiency of the two current systems. A pilot program for COA 3 can address those questions.

Design of a Pilot Program

Without sufficient data on outcomes of accession medical screening processing systems, it will be challenging for policymakers to address fundamental questions about the relative effectiveness and efficiency of the two systems and how they would function as a hybrid system. Under the assumption of DoD adopting a hybrid model (COA 3), we outline a three-step process to design a pilot program based on a randomized control trial (RCT), whereby samples of enlisted and officer applicants would be randomly assigned to MEPS or Concorde contract locations at multiple sites across the United States.

The first step is to determine and develop measures for desired outputs and outcomes of the system. We outline three categories of outcomes (effectiveness, efficiency, and experience), and describe system outputs, which are direct and immediate products of the system's inputs and activities. Based on the outputs and outcomes, we outline the types of measures and metrics for the pilot program. Table S.2 provides a recommended set of measures by outcome category.

After measures are determined, the next step of the pilot program design is to calculate the number of participants (sample size) needed to meet the program objectives. Sample sizes depend on a number of factors, many of which are currently unknown (e.g., type of statistical analysis to be conducted). Based on a set of assumptions about the pilot program design, we recommend a sample size of 1,600 participants (800 enlisted and 800 officer) for the pilot program.

The last step involves strategically selecting the sites where the pilot will be conducted, and then randomly assigning participants to either the experimental or control group to allow comparisons. Those in the experimental group would get medical screenings in a system they would not normally use (e.g., DoDMERB for enlisted applicants),

Table S.2
Recommended Measures and Metrics for Pilot Program

Outcome Category	Measures and Metrics
Effectiveness	Accuracy: proportion of participants who separate from enlisted (basic and initial skills) training or from officer accession source due to existing-prior-to-service (EPTS) medical reasons
	Reliability: audit of medical information used to make qualification decisions
Efficiency	Timeliness: length of applicant processing time, average commuting times to exam sites
	Financial costs: medical screening costs per applicant
	Time and cost: number and types of steps or phases in process
Experience	Surveys, interviews, and/or focus groups with participants, recruiters, and accession sources

and the control group would receive its medical screening as usual (e.g., MEPS for enlisted applicants). The selection of experimental sites was guided by geographical characteristics (e.g., urban/rural, demographic diversity, socioeconomic status) and MEPS organizational characteristics (e.g., site size, efficiency) so that the sites are representative. Based on a cluster analysis of MEPS locations, we identified four MEPS that we recommend serve as the geographic hubs for the pilot program: Louisville, Kentucky; Springfield, Massachusetts; San Diego, California; and Cleveland, Ohio.

Although an RCT-based pilot program is recommended, it is important to note that the financial costs associated with pilot programs can vary considerably. The more that a pilot program needs to develop new measures, collect data on-site with participants, conduct sophisticated analyses, and work with stakeholders, the costlier the pilot program will be. Because of the costs associated with an RCT-based pilot program, DoD may wish to conduct a less formal pilot program by expanding the USMC OCC/PLC program to other accession sources (without requiring random assignment). We expect doing this kind of pilot program would reduce costs for logistics of assigning participants to experimental sites and costs associated with stakeholder engagement (especially if accession sources are not required to participate). However, costs associated with measurement development, data collection, and data analysis would remain if DoD wished to evaluate the outcomes of the expanded program.

Recommendations

Based on the findings in this study, we offer two related recommendations for DoD to consider if they wish to change the business models for accession medical screening processing systems: (1) Adopt a hybrid model (COA 3) but also conduct pilot programs to test the model, and (2) ensure conditions are favorable for pilot program success.

Test and Adopt a Hybrid Model

Although each COA would impact DoDMERB's and USMEPCOM's business models for accession medical screening processing systems, COA 3 presents less risk than the other two COAs, as it does not require significant disruptions to either system's organizational structures and staffing; it has a template in the USMC OCC/PLC program; and it allows simultaneous testing of cross-flows of enlisted and officer applicants across the two systems.

We recommend COA 3 but also that it be tested before full implementation. We propose that DoD conduct one or more pilot programs along the lines we describe in this report. An RCT will provide the most complete answers to fundamental questions about the relative effectiveness and efficiency of the two systems. However, even an RCT can fail if conditions are not favorable for pilot program success—hence, our second recommendation.

Ensure Conditions Are Favorable for Pilot Program Success

DoD needs to heed lessons from past attempts at reform to ensure that the pilot program can succeed. Lessons include: clear articulation of the objectives for the pilot program to key stakeholders to ensure buy-in; continuity in leadership throughout the course of the pilot program's development and implementation; and an understanding of how the pilot program could affect other areas of reform. In particular, new information-sharing systems (e.g., electronic health systems and database management) would ideally be in place by the time a pilot program is launched, but if that is not the case, DoD would need to establish alternative information-sharing arrangements in the pilot program. We also recommend that our assumptions and estimates for the pilot program be revalidated, particularly if significant changes occur to either accession medical screening system before the pilot program is launched.

The costs of developing and implementing an RCT-based pilot program may also be a consideration, and DoD may choose a less costly pilot program design or forgo a pilot program in favor of continued reforms within the existing systems. However, any pilot program would incur costs to implement and evaluate, and some of DoD's ongoing efforts to improve the system may be costly. Moreover, a simpler pilot program design or staying the course with ongoing reform efforts may not sufficiently address key objectives for an updated and modernized accession medical screening system.

In conclusion, an RCT should give policymakers considerable insight into whether significant changes to the accession medical screening systems could result in a more effective and efficient hybrid system that can be introduced nationwide to all branches of the services.

Acknowledgments

Many people made this project a success. We begin by thanking our sponsor, Stephanie Miller, Director of Accession Policy in the Office of the Under Secretary of Defense for Personnel and Readiness/Military Personnel Policy (OUSD/P&R/MPP), for her support throughout the study. We also express gratitude to Chris Arendt (Deputy Director), Dennis Drogo (Assistant Director), Evelyn Dyer, and a former action officer, MAJ Kevin Bentz, who assisted our efforts.

Several individuals throughout DoD deserve our gratitude. We thank CAPT David Kemp, Director of USMEPCOM, for providing his time and that of his staff to educate us on USMEPCOM's mission, policies, procedures, and practices. From USMEPCOM we are especially thankful to Annette Waddelow for arranging our visit to USMEPCOM and acting as a subject matter expert and liaison for the project. We are very grateful to Larry Mullen, Deputy Director of DoDMERB, who is a font of knowledge on all things DoDMERB, both past and present. We also thank the subject matter experts from military accession sources (service academies, ROTCs, recruiting organizations) who provided invaluable inputs to the study. We especially thank the recruiters who provided inputs on their experiences with medical screening processes for their recruits. We cannot express our appreciation enough to the participants at our September 2017 workshop. Their knowledge and engagement made the workshop a resounding success.

We also extend our thanks to representatives of the U.S. Marine Corps Recruiting Command, including CAPT Scott Kates and MAJ Stephen Reamy, for providing data and approvals so we could access and analyze the data for the study. We also thank MAJ Celina Counce at USMEPCOM, as well as Donna Najar at the Defense Health Agency (DHA), for pulling data to support the analysis.

Finally, we offer our appreciation to current and former RAND colleagues, including John Winkler and Lisa Harrington, the Director and Associate Director of the Forces and Resources Policy Center (FRP), for their guidance throughout the project. Our former colleague Gail Fisher provided logistical and substantive support early in the project. We also thank two Army Medical Department (AMEDD) fellows at RAND, LTC Elba Villacorta and MAJ John (Joe) Pena, who provided insights on recruiting and screening of medical professionals through Officer Candidate School. Christopher Maerzluft built the geographic information system (GIS) tool to the team's specifications, and Ken Kuhn conducted analyses in support of the project's pilot program design. Spencer Case reviewed and summarized policy and procedural materials on the medical screening processes and worked diligently with Lemenuel Dungey, Clara Aranibar, and Will Mackenzie to organize the workshop and to take and clean notes. Agnes Schaefer provided invaluable quality assurance support throughout the project, and Curt Gilroy offered useful insights on drafts of the report. Melissa Bauman edited and revised an earlier version of this report to make it more streamlined and engaging to readers.

Abbreviations

ACMO	assistant chief medical officer
AMEDD	Army Medical Department
AMSWG	Accession Medical Standards Working Group
AMWG	Accession Modernization Working Group
ARNG	Army National Guard
ASD	Assistant Secretary of Defense
CMO	chief medical officer
COA	course of action
DADSIWG	Defense Accession Data Systems Integration Working Group
DASD	Deputy Assistant Secretary of Defense
DASD MPP	Deputy Assistant Secretary of Defense for Military Personnel Policy
DHA	Defense Health Agency
DoD	Department of Defense
DoDI	Department of Defense Instruction
DoDMERB	Department of Defense Medical Examination Review Board
DoDMETS	Department of Defense Medical Exam Testing System
DOTMLPF-P	Doctrine, Organization, Training, Materiel, Leadership/Education, Personnel, Facilities, and Policy

DUSD MPP	Deputy Under Secretary of Defense, Military Personnel Policy
EPTS	existing-prior-to-service
FY	fiscal year
GAO	Government Accountability Office
GIS	geographic information system
GMM	Gaussian Mixture Model
HAIMS	Health Artifact and Image Management Solution
HIV	human immunodeficiency virus
HTP	hometown providers
IG	inspector general
IT	information technology
JLV	Joint Legacy Viewer
MEDPERS	Medical and Personnel Executive Steering Committee
MEPS	Military Entrance Processing Station(s)
MHS	Military Health System
MPP	Military Personnel Policy
MTF	military treatment facility
NCO	noncommissioned officer
NDRI	National Defense Research Institute
NDS	National Defense Strategy
OCC	Officer Candidate Course
OUSD/P&R/MPP (AP)	Office of the Under Secretary of Defense for Personnel and Readiness/Military Personnel Policy, Accession Policy
OSD	Office of the Secretary of Defense
P&R IM	Personnel & Readiness Information Management
PLC	Platoon Leaders Class

RCT	randomized control trial
RHRP	Reserve Health Readiness Program
ROTC	Reserve Officers' Training Corps
SME	subject matter expert
SMWRA	Service Medical Waiver Review Authority
SPAWAR	Space and Naval Warfare Systems Command
USAREC	U.S. Army Recruiting Command
USMC	U.S. Marine Corps
USMC OCC/PLC	U.S. Marine Corps Officer Candidate Course/Platoon Leaders Class
USMEPCOM	U.S. Military Entrance Processing Command
USMIRS	USMEPCOM's Integrated Resource System
USUHS	Uniformed Services University of the Health Sciences

CHAPTER ONE

Introduction

Every year, the U.S. military processes over 300,000 applicants to determine their eligibility to serve. A key component of the entry screening process is evaluating applicants' medical fitness for military service. Although all military applicants must meet the medical requirements listed in the Department of Defense Instruction (DoDI) 6130.03, *Medical Standards for Appointment, Enlistment, or Induction into the Military Services,* two Department of Defense (DoD) organizations—the U.S. Military Entrance Processing Command (USMEPCOM) and the Department of Defense Medical Examination Review Board (DoDMERB)—oversee the medical screening of most of these applicants.[1]

Each organization has its own system for accession medical processing. Each also reports to a different DoD leader: USMEPCOM falls under the Director of Accession Policy within the Office of the Under Secretary of Defense for Personnel and Readiness/Military Personnel Policy (ODUSD/P&R/MPP); and DoDMERB falls under the Defense Health Agency (DHA), which reports to the Assistant Secretary of Defense (ASD) for Health Affairs. Ultimately, however, the responsibility for both enlisted and officer accessions falls to DASD MPP AP.

---

[1] Military Treatment Facilities (MTFs) are used to medically screen some applicants, such as a subset of medical professionals commissioning as Army officers. However, this report focuses on the two main organizations that provide accessions medical screening, DoDMERB and USMEPCOM.

In addition to overseeing other enlisted entrance processing activities (e.g., aptitude testing, biometrics assessment, oaths of enlistment), USMEPCOM oversees enlisted applicants' on-site medical screening (in addition to other entrance requirements) at one of 65 Military Entrance Processing Stations (MEPS) in the United States. Near the end of fiscal year (FY) 2018, over 396 MEPS medical personnel administered more than 305,000 medical examinations (USMEPCOM, undated).[2] Although USMEPCOM deals primarily with enlistment applicants, it does provide medical screening to some officer applicants, including special category officer applicants (e.g., direct commissions such as health care professionals) and many of those who would attend Officer Candidate School/Officer Training School.

DoDMERB oversees the medical screening of officer applicants for the U.S. military service academies, Reserve Officers' Training Corps (ROTC) scholarship programs, and Uniformed Services University of the Health Sciences (USUHS), among others.[3] With over 400 contracted medical exam locations dispersed throughout the United States, contract medical providers examine upward of 30,000 academically qualified officer applicants each year.[4]

Not only are the medical examinations these organizations oversee numerous, but the quality of the services these organizations provide also has a direct impact on the recruiting and readiness of the U.S. Armed Forces. As DoD has increased the end strength of the armed forces during a period of low civilian unemployment in recent years,

---

[2] As discussed later in this report, a majority of MEPS medical personnel are medical technicians, not physicians. At MEPS, government physicians are either chief medical officers (CMOs) or assistant CMOs (ACMOs). Each MEPS has only one CMO position, and several MEPS also have one ACMO position. In addition to government physicians, USMEPCOM contracts health providers based on daily projections of applicants requiring examinations.

[3] As of 2019, DoDMERB provides medical examination services to the following: military service academies, U.S. and state maritime academies, ROTC programs, USUHS, U.S. Army Judge Advocate General's Corps, U.S. Marine Corps Officer Candidate Course (OCC) and Platoon Leaders Course (PLC), and Public Health Service.

[4] These estimates were provided by a DoDMERB representative in February 2019. The number of applicants and contract exam locations varies from year to year. Each location that provides an initial medical examination includes a medical doctor, an optometrist, and in some cases, an audiologist.

the services aim to retain everyone who is dedicated and qualified to serve through the recruiting process. At the same time, they aim to identify someone who is not medically fit for military service early in the accession process, as attrition that occurs after individuals enter service can be extremely costly and hinder the services' ability to meet their recruiting missions and their mandated end strength.

Two Main Systems for Accession Medical Screening Processing

In the 1970s, DoD engaged in various accessions reforms. Many of them followed the establishment of the All-Volunteer Force in 1973, which required the services to recruit volunteers instead of relying on the draft. As part of its reform efforts, DoD stood up DoDMERB and USMEPCOM (formerly known as U.S. Military Enlistment Command). With those two organizations came two different systems for accession medical screening processes. We briefly describe the background of DoDMERB and USMEPCOM below, relying mainly on information that subject matter experts (SMEs) at DoDMERB and USMEPCOM provided to RAND in February and March 2019.

DoDMERB
In 1972, DoD established DoDMERB (then known as Service Academies Medical Examination Review Board) at the behest of the three military service academies (U.S. Military Academy [West Point], U.S. Naval Academy, and U.S. Air Force Academy). The academies' leadership wanted a comprehensive medical examination for applicants and based that medical examination on flight examinations for aircrew. Because of the availability of space for housing DoDMERB and proximity to flight surgeons, DoDMERB was headquartered at the U.S. Air Force Academy, where it still resides. At the time, the Office of the Secretary of Defense (OSD), Health Affairs, had policy oversight; the Air Force was an executive agent; and the Air Force Surgeon General had operational oversight of DoDMERB.

Over the years, other applicant sources have been added to DoDMERB's mission: ROTC scholarship (1975); USUHS (1976); ROTC nonscholarship (1998); U.S. Army Medical Department (AMEDD), Army Judge Advocate General's Corps, and Chaplain Corps (2008)[5]; U.S. Marine Corps Officer Candidate Course (OCC)/Platoon Leaders Class (PLC) (2013); and Public Health Service (2018).[6] DoDMERB's services have evolved over time as well. For example, in 1998, DoDMERB was authorized to pay for additional consults and tests needed to complete DoDMERB qualification decisions and waiver decisions.

USMEPCOM

In 1976, DoD established the U.S. Military Enlistment Processing Command to oversee enlistment accessions across the services (Johnson, 2008). According to information provided by a USMEPCOM representative in March 2019, the command was formed with structural elements of the U.S. Army Recruiting Command (USAREC) and the Air Force Vocational Testing Group. At the time, the commander of USAREC also served as commander of the U.S. Military Enlistment Processing Command (which may explain why the U.S. Army is executive agent of USMEPCOM and the important role of recruiters at MEPS). Although specifics about the history of medical screening processes at MEPS were not provided to RAND, it stands to reason that each MEPS would include a medical screening function as part of USMEPCOM's mission to oversee the common elements of entrance processing across the military services.

Summary

DoDMERB and USMEPCOM were established at a time of significant reforms in military accessions processes. However, they were established to meet different needs. DoDMERB arose out of a specific

---

[5]   According to a DoDMERB representative in 2019, AMEDD and chaplain applicants no longer go through DoDMERB.

[6]   Although the USMC OCC/PLC program began in 2010, it was not until 2013 that OSD officially directed DoDMERB to provide exams to the program.

desire by the military service academies for a rigorous medical screening process for applicants, while USMEPCOM was established to provide oversight of enlistment processing (not just medical screening) across the services. The two medical screening systems evolved in parallel along with their organizations, although both organizations have worked together to set medical standards and identify ways to standardize certain features of their systems (e.g., exam forms).

Study Objective and Background

The OUSD/P&R/MPP (AP), which is responsible for DoD recruiting and accession policies and programs for both officers and the enlisted force, asked RAND's National Defense Research Institute (NDRI) to examine the current officer and enlisted military service accession medical screening systems,[7] with the objective of developing options for an updated and improved system that may include conducting a pilot program at experimental sites.[8] We identify five questions in our project:

- What are key features of the current accession medical screening systems?
- What do stakeholders consider as challenges with these two systems?
- What efforts have been considered or made to improve these systems?
- What are options for changing the business models of the current systems, and what are potential trade-offs of those options?

---

[7] Throughout this report, we refer to USMEPCOM and DoDMERB systems because USMEPCOM does process some officer applicants.

[8] Our study did not involve a cost analysis to identify specific efficiencies that could be gained within the current systems, since our focus was on the implications of changing the business models for the two systems. However, in Chapter 3, we highlight past and ongoing efforts in DoD to improve the current systems, which include activities that may drive efficiencies in them.

- What are key considerations for conducting one or more pilot programs to test options for changing the business models of the current systems?

By exploring the five questions, our project aims to provide OSD with a means to implement guidance from the 2018 National Defense Strategy (NDS) of the United States of America, which emphasizes a culture of performance based on the effective stewardship of tax-payer resources (DoD, 2018). The NDS states that "delivering performance means we will shed outdated management practices and structures while integrating insights from business innovation" (DoD, 2018, p. 10). It also instructs "Service Secretaries and Agency heads to consolidate, eliminate, or restructure as needed" any current structures that are found to be inefficient and a hindrance to improving performance (DoD, 2018, p. 10). Finally, NDS states: "The Department's leadership is committed to changes in authorities, granting of waivers, and securing external support for streamlining processes and organizations" (DoD, 2018, p. 10).

Modifying the business models of the two accession medical screening systems has the potential to meet the strategic goals that the NDS describes. Both systems adhere to the same medical requirements listed in DoDI 6130.03. Both systems also have national footprints designed to maximize their accessibility for military applicants across the country. Although similar, each system has important differences that we outline later in the report. These differences make it challenging to assess the causal impact of a possible change in the business models of these two systems without a rigorous evaluation of systematically collected data.

Fortunately, there are established laws and regulations on how federal agencies might design and implement such an evaluation. As the U.S. Accountability Office (GAO) notes, "The Government Performance and Results Act of 1993 (GPRA) and the GPRA Modernization Act of 2010 (GPRAMA) were intended to provide both congressional and executive decisionmakers with objective information on the relative effectiveness and efficiency of federal programs and spending" (GAO, 2017, p. 1). For a few decades, GAO and the

Office of Management and Budget have recommended that federal government agencies implement rigorous program evaluation efforts to "improve the efficiency and effectiveness of limited government resources" (GAO, 2017).

Based on the 2010 act, GAO defines program evaluations as "systematic studies that use research methods to address specific questions about program performance" (GAO, 2013, p. 4). As GAO (2013, p. 4) notes,

> Policy makers can use evaluation results to (1) clarify understanding of how the program does or does not address a problem of interest, (2) make changes to improve the design or management of an existing program or policy, (3) support or change resource allocations within or across programs, (4) share promising practices or lessons learned with service provider or program partners, or (5) improve the quality of program or policy assessment.

"In particular," GAO states, "evaluations can be designed to isolate the causal impact of programs from other external economic or environmental conditions in order to assess a program's effectiveness" (GAO, 2013, p. 4). Following the federal regulations and standards, we adopt the principles of program evaluation in our design of the pilot program to estimate the impact of screening officer applicants by USMEPCOM's medical providers at MEPS instead of by DoDMERB's contracted medical providers.

Study Approach

Operationally, we applied qualitative as well as quantitative methods to accomplish the study objective. We conducted focus groups with enlisted recruiters and discussions with approximately 35 stakeholders from the Accession Medical Working Group (AMWG), DoD Health Affairs, DoDMERB, OUSD/P&R/MPP (AP), officer accession sources (service academies, ROTC programs), service medical waiver authorities, USMEPCOM, AMEDD, and USAREC to learn about current policies and practices and to identify challenges associated with the accession medical screening systems.[9] We also reviewed reform efforts to improve these systems' efficiency and effectiveness, focusing on available documentation (e.g., briefing slides) provided by DoDMERB and USMEPCOM on past reform efforts directed by leadership in DoD and on information on current efforts from interviews with representatives from DoDMERB, USMEPCOM, AMWG, and OUSD/P&R/MPP (AP). Our aim in reviewing past and current reform efforts was to identify what DoD and the services have tried (and are trying) to change about the systems, the types of challenges faced in making such changes, and how DoD might address such challenges if the goal is to reform the business models of the two systems.

Based on our reviews and stakeholder discussions, we identified three main courses of action (COAs) for modifying the structure and organization of resources and activities (i.e., the business models) used by USMEPCOM and DoDMERB for accession medical screening processing. We also developed criteria to assess the potential impact of fully executing each COA.

Next, we provided guidance for designing and executing pilot program(s) that can help DoD determine whether the COA we identify as the one to adopt can meet the intended outcomes for an updated accession medical screening system. We used the aforementioned GAO guidance on program evaluation to frame the general discussion on pilot program design; and supplemented it with details on the measures and metrics to use, the sample sizes required, and geographic locations that would be suitable. To get information that would allow us to provide these design details, we conducted a design workshop as well as developed and applied a logic model and interactive tool to examine methodological considerations for site selection.

---

[9]   We held discussions with a small number of representatives from the U.S. Army Medical Department (AMEDD) and U.S. Army Recruiting Command (USAREC) to learn about recruiting and medical screening for Army officers who are accessed through AMEDD. Unlike service academies and ROTCs, which send officer applicants through DoDMERB, AMEDD typically sends its officer applicants through MEPS for accessions medical screening. We use discussions about AMEDD applicants as an illustrative example of experiences for officer applicants going through MEPS versus other medical screening systems. We also highlight a previous pilot effort in Chapter 3.

- **Design workshop with key stakeholders:** In September 2017, we conducted a workshop with 23 SMEs representing key stakeholders of the two accession medical screening systems. The objectives of the workshop were to (1) determine the key strategic elements of the pilot for evaluation purposes and (2) shape a site selection procedure for the pilot program.
- **Detailed logic model of an accession medical screening system:** Based on workshop feedback, our review of the current systems, and the literature on program evaluation, we developed a detailed logic model depicting how the components of the system interact, which is the typical starting point for program evaluation.
- **Geographic information system (GIS) interactive tool:** We analyzed data on MEPS features (e.g., size), MEPS and DoDMERB contract provider locations, and applicant zip codes in the tool to (1) estimate the amount of time it takes applicants to drive to MEPS or DoDMERB contract exam locations, and (2) analyze MEPS features to identify groups (clusters) of MEPS for experimental sites in a pilot program.

We conclude our study with recommendations based on our review of the current accession medical screening systems, ongoing and past reform efforts, and scientific literature on program evaluation, as well as the COAs that we developed and assessed for potential impacts on DoDMERB and USMEPCOM's accession medical screening systems.[10]

Organization of the Report

The structure of the report reflects our approach. Chapter 2 describes the current systems for accession medical screening processes and their potential challenges, as well as the relative advantages and disad-

---

[10] RAND's Institutional Review Board (the Human Subjects Protection Committee) determined that this study is "Not Research Involving Human Subjects," in accordance with appropriate federal statutes and DoD regulations governing human subjects protection.

vantages of the two systems. Chapter 3 summarizes current and past reform efforts to improve the accession medical screening systems, including past attempts to modify the business models underlying the two systems. In Chapter 4, we outline three main COAs for reforming the business models used for the two systems, assess the potential impact of each COA on DoDMERB and USMEPCOM, and select one COA for recommended adoption by DoD. Chapter 5 provides a detailed description of key elements of pilot program design. In Chapter 6 we summarize key findings and offer specific recommendations for DoD to consider to update the accession screening systems.

We also provide four appendices to supplement the main report. Appendix A describes our methodology for stakeholder discussions. Appendix B provides the methodology for the design workshop. Appendix C describes a detailed logic model for an accession screening system. Finally, Appendix D offers a more technical discussion of the cluster analysis used as part of the pilot program design in Chapter 5.

CHAPTER TWO

Overview of Accession Medical Screening Systems, Their Potential Challenges, and Their Relative Advantages and Disadvantages

In this chapter, we first describe the current systems for accession medical screening processes employed by DoDMERB and USMEPCOM and then discuss different types of challenges with those processes that were raised by key stakeholders in interviews and focus groups. Stakeholders include USMEPCOM, DoDMERB, USMEPCOM's organizational "customers" (e.g., enlisted recruiters, AMEDD recruiting), and DoDMERB's organizational "customers" (i.e., military service academies and ROTCs).

Current Processes in the Two Systems

The following sections provide a high-level overview of the USMEPCOM and DoDMERB medical screening process steps. Most of the information is current as of 2017, and some information is from USMEPCOM regulations published in 2018.

USMEPCOM Medical Screening Processes

USMEPCOM is a major command in the U.S. military and oversees entrance processing for military enlistment, not just medical screening. USMEPCOM oversees MEPS, which are the "one-stop" locations for enlistment processing: aptitude and other entrance testing required by the services, biometrics assessment (mainly to identify applicants), job placement guidance (by the services), medical screening, and oaths of enlistment.

In terms of medical screening processes, USMEPCOM determines whether enlisted applicants and special category officer applicants (i.e., people with direct commissions such as health care professionals, chaplains, and attorneys) are medically qualified for service and meet service- and job-specific medical standards (USMEPCOM Regulation 40-1, 2018). USMEPCOM also processes Officer Candidate School/Officer Training School applicants and can process ROTC applicants.

Prescreening

Applicants must complete multiple prescreening steps before an in-person MEPS medical exam. All prescreening medical examination forms are done on paper. Recruiters work with applicants to complete a prescreening medical form (valid for 90 days)[1] and collect supporting medical documents identified in the prescreening form, such as applicable historical medical and treatment records (USMEPCOM Regulation 601-23, 2017; USMEPCOM Regulation 40-1, 2018). The recruiting services/commands submit the applicant packet to the MEPS medical department for processing. Recruiters can also connect directly to the MEPS medical department through the Dial-A-Doc/Email-A-Doc Program to ask questions about applicant medical conditions/problems. In the event of a medical disqualification, recruiters can submit medical waivers to their respective service for review.

The MEPS chief medical officer (CMO), assistant CMO (ACMO), or the MEPS contracted provider approves the applicant's medical packets and returns the documents to the applicant's service liaison with a determination about applicant qualification and any requests for additional documentation or waivers (USMEPCOM Regulation 40-1, 2018). MEPS medical noncommissioned officers (NCOs) in charge/supervisory medical technicians ("med-techs") ensure the quality of medical packets. Med-techs review questions without "yes" responses regarding an applicant's medical history on the medical prescreening

---

[1]   The prescreening medical form is DoD Form 2807-2, *Accessions Medical Prescreen Report*.

forms. Depending on the number of "yes" responses to previous/current medical conditions, the MEPS medical department is allowed upward of three days to process the medical prescreening form.[2]

When an applicant is cleared to continue processing, he or she is scheduled for a MEPS physical (USMEPCOM Regulation 40-1, 2018). If the applicant is not approved, the MEPS medical department files a case for the applicant and notifies the service liaison. Applicants with incomplete medical records are given an "open for records" status, and the medical process stops until complete medical records are provided to the MEPS medical department.

As part of the medical prescreening process, a med-tech manually enters all applicant data into USMEPCOM's Integrated Resource System (USMIRS). USMIRS includes biographical information, medical profile details, disqualification data, and waiver approval details (National Research Council, 2006). USMIRS does not track medical disqualification data for applicants who do not pass through MEPS (USMEPCOM Regulation 680-3, 2006).

In-Person Medical Screening and Qualification Processes

Figure 2.1 outlines the major steps of the medical screening process at MEPS. About two days after the MEPS medical department provides the service liaison office with prescreen approval, applicants report to MEPS for processing.[3] For medical processing, applicants report to the medical department and check in at the control desk. Applicants receive a brief on the medical screening process and are then required to complete screening forms.

Once forms are complete, applicants go through a series of medical screening tests and evaluations. Applicants undergo hearing and vision tests, typically with med-techs. Applicants also undergo interviews and exams with MEPS medical providers, who are government civilians or

---

[2] The CMO can request additional time for more complex cases.

[3] Enlisted recruits receive support to complete processing. MEPS provides lodging the night before and transportation to the MEPS the day of the visit. MEPS operations officers are responsible for applicant flow through the MEPS process, as well as ensuring that the medical processing is complete and that applicant data are entered in USMIRS (USMEPCOM Regulation 601-23, 2017; USMEPCOM Regulation 40-1, 2018).

Figure 2.1
USMEPCOM In-Person Medical Screening Activities

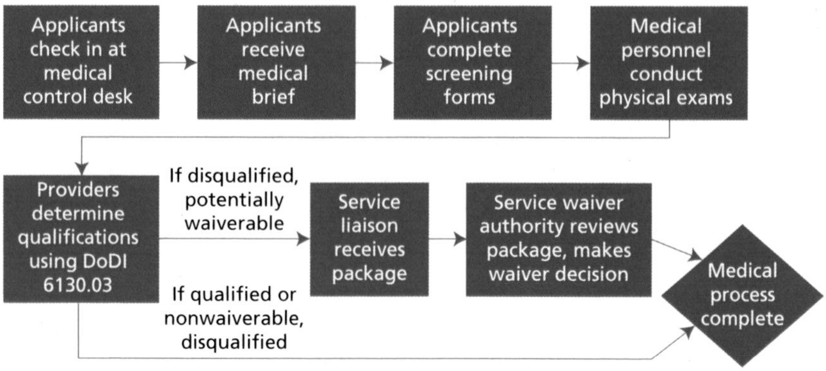

SOURCE: USMEPCOM Regulations 40-1 (2018) and 601-23 (2017).

contract health providers (i.e., fee-based providers). Applicants receive orthopedic/neurological exams individually or in groups of up to eight people.[4] Each applicant also participates in a medical history interview, in which the medical provider asks questions about the applicant's medical history based on information and prescreening forms that the applicant had provided (Personnel & Readiness Information Management [P&R IM], 2015).[5] MEPS medical providers also conduct one-on-one medical exams, which include measuring blood pressure/pulse rate and height/weight/body fat, as well as collecting a blood/urine specimen to test for conditions such as human immunodeficiency virus (HIV), drugs and alcohol, and pregnancy (USMEPCOM Regulation 601-23, 2017; USMEPCOM Regulation 40-1, 2018).[6]

---

[4]   The orthopedic/neurological exams inform an applicant's physical profile, including physical capacity, upper extremities, lower extremities, hearing and ears, and psychiatric.

[5]   MEPS health providers review two main forms. One is DoD Form 2807-1, *Report of Medical History*, which helps the provider determine if the applicant needs any focused exams (USMEPCOM Regulation 40-1, 2018). The other is DoD Form 2807-2, *Accessions Medical Prescreen Report*.

[6]   Medical examination results are reported on DoD Form 2808, *Report of Medical Examination* (2005). The exam information on this form is considered valid for two years.

Once medical screening is complete, a government or certified-contract provider determines whether each applicant screened at that MEPS meets the medical qualifications for military service in DoDI 6130.03 (USMEPCOM Regulation 601-23, 2017; USMEPCOM Regulation 40-1, 2017).[7] The MEPS medical screening process is designed to be completed in one day if the applicant is medically qualified or is medically disqualified and not able to receive a waiver (USMEPCOM Regulation 601-23, 2017). A med-tech enters all screening and physical exam data into USMIRS (USMEPCOM Regulation 40-1, 2017).

If the MEPS provider determines that a medically disqualified applicant might be eligible for a medical waiver, the MEPS medical section sends the applicant's package for waiver review. The package goes to the MEPS's liaison for the military service that the applicant is trying to enter (e.g., Army). The service liaison is responsible for submitting the package for waiver review to the Service Medical Waiver Review Authority (SMWRA) for that military service. SMWRA decides whether the applicant is medically qualified (i.e., the disqualifying condition is "waiverable"), requires additional documentation or consultation, or is medically disqualified, at which time the medical process is complete (USMEPCOM Regulation 601-23, 2017; USMEPCOM Regulation 40-1, 2018). The waiver review process is meant to be completed by the next business day after the MEPS medical section submits the package for SMWRA waiver review.

DoDMERB Medical Screening Processes

Unlike USMEPCOM, which oversees enlistment processing overall, DoDMERB's primary mission is to provide medical examinations to determine medical qualifications for service, with a focus on officer accessions. DoDMERB medical screening processes include the fol-

---

[7] MEPS CMOs train and certify contract providers. There are four certification levels known as Designated Provider Categories (DPCs). Contract providers who reach DPC Level 3 can "profile" applicants to make qualification determinations. Providers who reach DPC Level 4 can temporarily perform the duties of the CMO if the government CMO or ACMO is not available. However, the government CMO is ultimately responsible for the certification of the contract providers and the accuracy of applicants' profiles (USMEPCOM, 40-1, 2017).

lowing major steps: scheduling medical exams, appraising evaluation assessments, determining whether applicants are medically qualified or disqualified, and maintaining medical files/examination data (P&R IM, 2015). DoDMERB contracts with Concorde Inc., which executes key steps in the process.[8] However, DoDMERB staff make the medical qualification determinations.[9]

Figure 2.2 depicts the key steps in the DoDMERB process, and we describe them below.

Prescreening

For the three military service academies, the academy admissions office recommends which of its applicants should receive medical screening. According to our discussions with admissions office representatives, the office forwards an applicant for medical screening if that individual has already completed the first or second phase of the academy's application process and is deemed competitive after an initial academic screening. For the ROTC programs, scholarship applicants or those with advanced standing also need to complete screening through DoDMERB. Nonscholarship applicants not in advanced standing may not need medical screening (at least not through DoDMERB) unless/until they reach advanced standing (P&R IM, 2015).

Applicants recommended for medical screening are referred to DoDMERB,[10] which emails applicants with directions on scheduling the medical exams and completing the online prescreening forms (i.e.,

---

[8] Concorde Inc. provides officer applicants going through DoDMERB with access to the necessary medical personnel to complete their medical requirements, including medical exams (Concorde Inc., 2018).

[9] Based on discussions and input from a DoDMERB SME in 2016, the director of DoDMERB is a military officer (O-6) from one of the military services. DoDMERB includes several medical professional staff, an optometrist, several operational staff, and administrative staff (mainly for records management). Medical professional staff conduct the medical qualification reviews.

[10] According to information provided by a DoDMERB SME in 2019, the services send an electronic "tasker" to DoDMERB for the applicants whom they require to be screened. An exception to this process is for ROTC applicants on college campuses. These applicants are sent directly to Concorde. However, Concorde's system checks to see if the applicant has a valid DoDMERB exam for a previous national-level application (e.g., for a service academy).

Figure 2.2
DoDMERB Medical Screening Processes for Academy and Reserve Officer Training Corps Applicants

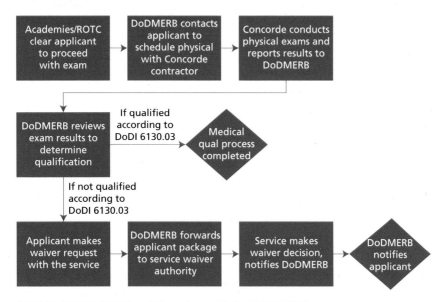

SOURCE: P&R IM (2015) and discussions with DoDMERB SMEs.
NOTE: An exception to the second step of the process exists for ROTC applicants who are based on college campuses. These applicants can go directly into the Concorde system for scheduling their examinations without waiting for letters from DoDMERB.

medical history questions) through the DoD Medical Exam Testing System (DoDMETS) (P&R IM, 2015).[11]

In-Person Medical Screening and Qualification Processes

Concorde arranges and conducts the medical exams and reports results to DoDMERB. Applicants travel to the Concorde medical exam pro-

---

If the applicant has a valid exam, the system automatically rejects the applicant's request for a new exam.

[11] DoDMETS is the medical exam tracking system operated by Concorde Inc. It assists applicants in scheduling and completing their medical requirements for DoDMERB. In DoDMETS, applicants can complete the required medical information questions, log their appointment times and dates, and track the status of their medical requirements (Concorde Inc., 2018).

viders. Most medical exams (about 90 percent) are conducted by contract civilian medical examiners (P&R IM, 2015), who are medical professionals hired by Concorde and trained to conduct accession medical exams in the DoDMERB system. These contract providers are dispersed around the United States for easier access by applicants. Alternatively, exams are carried out at military treatment facilities (MTFs). DoDMERB pays for initial medical examinations, which include the full clinical evaluation, as well as vision and hearing tests.[12] DoDMERB does not require or pay for drug, alcohol, or HIV testing (P&R IM, 2015). Unlike the military services, which pay for enlisted applicants' meals and lodging when they visit MEPS, DoDMERB does not cover the costs of applicants' transportation, lodging, or other incidentals (P&R IM, 2015).

The determination of medical qualification is not made on the same day of the examination (P&R IM, 2015). Instead, Concorde medical examiners print and mail the completed medical assessment, medical history, and statement of present health forms to DoDMERB for review (P&R IM, 2015).[13] In addition, DoDMERB refers to results from 13 additional questionnaires that have been completed by the applicants and provide information on specific areas of health (e.g., headaches, insomnia, and orthopedics) (P&R IM, 2015). DoDMERB personnel scan all medical exam forms and enter the data into DoDMERB's database for maintaining and monitoring applicants' medical screening information (P&R IM, 2015). Then, DoDMERB medical staff review exam results and determine whether applicants meet the medical qualifications stipulated in DoDI 6130.03 (P&R IM, 2015). According to DoDMERB (2016), there are three types of medical qualification determinations: (1) qualified, (2) remedial (i.e., addi-

---

[12] Applicants may be required to receive an additional exam by an optometrist/ophthalmologist, which includes the Red Lens Test, the Farnsworth Lantern Test, and the Red/Green Color Vision Test. A dental examination is also required (P&R IM, 2015).

[13] The forms (in order of reference) are DoD Form 2351, *DoD Medical Examination Review Board Report of Medical Examination*; DoD Form 2492, *DoD Medical Examination Review Board Report of Medical History*; and, DoD Form 2372, *DoD Medical Examination Review Board Statement of Present Health*. The medical exam and medical histories are valid for two years (P&R IM, 2015).

tional test/medical records are required), or (3) does not meet DoD medical standards. Disqualified applicants can request medical waivers from their respective service.

Academy admissions offices or ROTC detachment or battalion commanders, initiate the waiver process for applicants deemed competitive (DoDMERB, 2016). According to a DoDMERB SME who provided input in 2016, DoDMERB now forwards applicant packages to the respective service waiver authorities and command surgeons. The command surgeons make the waiver decisions and notify DoDMERB. The services must go back through DoDMERB to request additional paperwork during the waiver process. After the service makes a final determination, DoDMERB reports back to the applicant and the officer program organization (e.g., the service academy), and the organization also sends a decision letter to the applicant.

Difficulties in Comparing the Two Systems
Because USMEPCOM and DoDMERB employ different business models for accession medical screening, the resources they require for medical screening differ substantially. Although there is some overlap with the officer applicants who go to MEPS, they serve populations that differ significantly in terms of size (and perhaps in terms of medical conditions). They also offer different levels of support and services to applicants and use varying numbers and types of examination locations and personnel. Moreover, the two organizations are not similarly sized or scoped: DoDMERB's mission is to provide medical examination reviews whereas USMEPCOM's mission is "determining the physical, mental and moral qualifications of every member of the armed services" (USMEPCOM, undated). That is, USMEPCOM oversees enlisted screening processes (e.g., aptitude testing) writ large.

As we discuss in the next chapter, analysis to compare the costs of examinations across the two systems is challenging because of these differences. Therefore, rather than offering a direct comparison of the costs for the two systems, we provide a table summarizing the type and levels of staffing (including contract support) used by the two systems (Table 2.1). The estimates of government staffing levels are based on the number of positions (billets) that DoDMERB and USMEPCOM are authorized to have, which is larger than the actual size of its current staff. Contract health provider estimates are rough approximations based on information given by DoDMERB and USMEPCOM representatives in February and March 2019. However, the number of contract health providers will vary based on system demands (i.e., number of applicants by location).

As Table 2.1 shows, staffing differs markedly between the two systems. Not surprisingly, DoDMERB has relatively few government employees (approximately 34 positions) but contracts hundreds of health providers through Concorde. The initial screening examinations are conducted at 420 locations, with each site including one medical doctor and one optometrist and some including audiologists.

USMEPCOM, in comparison, employs hundreds of government staff across MEPS medical sections, including medical professionals (CMOs, ACMOs), medical/health care NCOs, and med-techs. Based on authorizations data provided by USMEPCOM in March 2019, MEPS medical sections have, on average, ten personnel (standard deviation = 3.9). In addition, there are eight government personnel at the two USMEPCOM sectors and 30 positions at USMEPCOM HQs in the Medical Plans and Policy Directorate (USMEPCOM J-7). In total, 668 government positions existed in the USMEPCOM accession medical screening system as of March 2019. These positions are augmented with contract health providers at MEPS sites, but the average number of contractors is much lower than in the DoDMERB system (140 versus 840).

Issues with Current Systems: Stakeholder Interviews and Focus Groups

We conducted interviews and focus groups with key stakeholders to learn about their concerns and perspectives.[14] (See Appendix A for a description of interview and focus group methodologies and samples.)

---

[14] Interviews were conducted from July 2016 through March 2017. Focus groups were conducted from March 2017 to January 2018. Changes made to USMEPCOM or DoDMERB processes in FY 2018 may not be reflected in stakeholders' comments.

Table 2.1
Staffing Estimates for DoDMERB and USMEPCOM Accession Medical Screening Systems

	Staff Type	Location Type	Estimated Staffing Levels	
			DoDMERB	**USMEPCOM**
Government staff (billets)	Physicians/ certified health providers	Exam locations	Not applicable (only contractors)	65 CMOs (civilian) 26 ACMOs (civilian)
		Higher-level organization[a]	5 physicians (4 military, 1 civilian) 16 reviewers (10 military, 6 civilian)	4 at sectors (2 per sector) 6 at headquarters (HQ) (2 military, 4 civilian)
	Medical/health care NCOs and med-techs	Exam locations	Not applicable	123 medical/ health care NCOs 416 med-techs[b] (civilian)
		Higher-level organization	8 med techs (civilian)	1 (military)
	Other staff (e.g., directors, supervisors, administrative support, analysts)	Higher-level organization	5 (mostly supervisory and civilian)[c]	4 at sectors (2 per sector) 23 at HQ (all but one are civilian)
Total government			**34**	**668**
Contract health providers		Exam locations	At least 840[d]	Daily average of 140[e]

NOTES: [a] Higher-level organization refers to nonexam sites in the system. For DoDMERB, this means DoDMERB HQ. For USMEPCOM, this means at sector level or at USMEPCOM HQ.

[b] Majority of med-techs (314 out of 416) are general schedule (GS) level 6 (GS-6) civilians. Only 19 med-tech billets are supervisory (GS-9), and 83 are lead med-techs (GS-7).

[c] In mid-2019, DHA will oversee contracted support at DoDMERB headquarters (e.g., IT administration). The number of personnel working at DoDMERB will likely change as a result.

[d] Each initial examination location has at least one medical doctor and one optometrist. Since there are 420 locations as of 2019, at least 840 (= 420 x 2) providers are in the system. However, 840 is an underestimate because some locations include audiologists.

[e] Estimate provided by USMEPCOM in March 2019. Numbers fluctuate daily based on expected numbers of applicants who require medical screenings at MEPS. Some contract providers can fill in for CMOs if those providers are certified by USMEPCOM to perform the temporary duties of a CMO.

We first spoke with USMEPCOM and DoDMERB representatives to learn about potential issues arising from a combined system and to ensure that we acknowledged their concerns. To explore these concerns further and identify other issues to consider, we conducted interviews and focus groups with enlisted recruiters and AMEDD recruiting representatives, whom we considered "customers" of the USMEPCOM and DoDMERB systems due to their experience with the processes and related outcomes of these systems.[15] We also interviewed admissions representatives from the service academies and ROTC programs to better understand potential issues with the DoDMERB system and explore any concerns about a combined system.[16]

It is important to note that interviews and focus groups are designed to be exploratory in nature and to provide greater context into potential issues surrounding the current medical systems. These qualitative data include individuals' opinions and perceptions that the study identifies as important for OSD to consider when exploring options for an updated accession medical screening system, but the methodology of this study did not allow for validation of all concerns raised by stakeholders.

USMEPCOM and DoDMERB Concerns About Combining the Accession Medical Process

When asked about the possibility of a combined accession medical system, representatives from both USMEPCOM and DoDMERB raised concerns about their respective enlisted and officer applicants receiving medical screening from the other's system. It is important to note, however, that while USMEPCOM and DoDMERB operate as

---

[15] Prior to conducting interviews and focus groups, the project team secured approval from RAND's Human Subjects Protection Committee, which prohibits the project team from naming individuals who participated (i.e., direct identification) or noting participants' characteristics in such a way that their identities could be readily inferred.

[16] The study team also conducted interviews with service waiver authorities, including U.S. Navy Bureau of Medicine and Surgery (BUMED) representatives, for additional context about current medical screening systems. Information from these discussions is not included in this section, as the focus of discussions was logistics of the waiver processes rather than opinions about the overall screening systems.

distinct systems, with each focused on a unique population of applicants, these two systems regularly collaborate and coordinate to promote effective enterprise-wide medical screening.

USMEPCOM Concerns

USMEPCOM representatives expressed a number of concerns related to enlisted applicants using the DoDMERB system. First, they were concerned about the ability to validate the quality of exams offered by DoDMERB's contract medical providers. USMEPCOM medical providers are trained in "accession medicine," defined as "evaluating the suitability of the moral, physical, and mental condition of prospective applicants for entry into military service," and USMEPCOM representatives see this as a unique capability of USMEPCOM medical departments (USMEPCOM, 2016, p. 22). They noted that DoDMERB's contractors are not trained in accession medicine to address military needs. While USMEPCOM also uses contracted medical providers, they are monitored and trained by DoD and work on-site under CMOs.

Additionally, USMEPCOM stakeholders raised concerns about hometown doctors potentially advocating for applicants who may not be qualified. For example, if an applicant is screened by his lifelong physician with whom he has developed a rapport, the physician may want the patient to achieve his goal of enlisting in the military and overlook a potentially disqualifying medical issue.

Due to the lack of training in accession medicine and the potential for hometown doctors to advocate for applicants, USMEPCOM representatives predicted increased enlistment of medically unfit recruits under the DoDMERB model. They believed that private medical providers would also be less able to identify nondisclosed health issues, whether nondisclosure was intentional or not, because those providers are not trained or accustomed to approaching medical screening in this manner. USMEPCOM representatives also think that certain medical issues—for example, mental health conditions related to self-harm—are more prevalent in the enlisted recruit population compared to the officer applicant population and that USMEPCOM medical personnel are better trained to identify such issues, which could signal an applicant is medically unfit to serve.

DoDMERB Concerns

We also interviewed DoDMERB representatives to gain their perspectives on a combined system. Like USMEPCOM representatives, DoDMERB stakeholders were concerned about their officer applicants using the USMEPCOM system rather than the current DoDMERB system. However, their concerns focused not on quality but on inconveniences and recruiting challenges that could result from the USMEPCOM system.

DoDMERB stakeholders pointed out that there are just 65 MEPS locations across the country, compared to Concorde's roughly 400 sites for DoDMERB exams. DoDMERB representatives emphasized that applicants far from a MEPS location would have significantly longer travel times—known as "windshield time"—to their medical screening appointment. This could potentially require an overnight stay or other travel expenses and additional time off work or school. DoDMERB representatives also noted that access to a MEPS location could prove difficult or unfeasible for applicants from rural areas far from a MEPS or without easy access to a vehicle. Additionally, they mentioned USMEPCOM's lack of an online appointment system, which would act as another inconvenience for applicants to navigate. DoDMERB believes these inconveniences and access issues could deter officer applicants from pursuing military service.

DoDMERB representatives were also concerned about exposing officer applicants to elements of enlisted military culture at MEPS, including their perceived "cattle calls" and "hurry up and wait" procedures, which officer applicants might find unexpected, off-putting, and unfamiliar, and which could deter them from pursuing further application steps.[17] Due to these inconveniences, access issues, and unfamiliar culture, DoDMERB representatives predicted that the service academies and ROTCs would face recruiting challenges under the USMEPCOM model. They had particular concerns about deterring elite officer applicants from pursuing military service. For example, if an applicant were deciding between entering the U.S. Air Force Acad-

---

[17] Later in this chapter we describe officer applicants' "VIP" or "red carpet" treatment experiences at some MEPS, which would address some of these concerns.

emy or an elite civilian university, these factors could drive the applicant toward the civilian university, where such inconveniences and environments do not apply.

Finally, DoDMERB representatives noted that, while Concorde physicians are not trained in accession medicine in the same manner as MEPCOM physicians, they are removed from the decisionmaking process and are simply recording results that are then provided to the military service for outcome decisions. DoDMERB representatives emphasized that Concorde physicians rarely have an existing relationship with the applicant and should be able to conduct exams in an objective manner.

USMEPCOM "Customer" Perspectives

To understand their experience with MEPS, we spoke with "customers" of USMEPCOM. This included focus groups with enlisted recruiters across the services and interviews with AMEDD recruiting representatives who represent a population of officer candidates currently using MEPS for medical screening. These discussions aimed to inform potential future efforts to update the accession medical screening system.

Enlisted Recruiters

Recruiters noted that medical processing through MEPS is unnecessarily time-consuming and slows down the recruitment process. They complained that assisting applicants with MEPS screenings and paperwork takes them away from other recruiting activities and cited medical processing as the main barrier to a timely recruitment process.

Recruiters also raised concerns about a lack of consistency across MEPS sites. Some recruiters drive applicants several extra hours to a MEPS location that they perceive to be more efficient or that qualifies applicants more frequently than the MEPS that is closest to them. Other recruiters said they wanted to drive to other MEPS locations for these reasons but are not able to use a MEPS site outside their district. Recruiters also noted a lack of consistency across medical cases, even within the same MEPS location. They mentioned that the required paperwork and waiver outcomes often varied for different applicants with the same medical issues. For example, recruiters described applicants who both had asthma and were told that they required different types of paperwork to document the medical issue and received different waiver determinations; the same occurred with applicants who had broken wrists in the past. While recruiters acknowledged that they are not medically trained to understand all the intricacies and potential differences of the cases, they noted that these inconsistencies make it difficult for them to prepare applicants for the medical screening process in terms of the documentation needed and expectations.

Recruiters also expressed frustration with a perceived lack of transparency and accountability in the MEPS process. Recruiters said they often find themselves fielding questions from applicants or their parents about the status of their medical processing. Once an applicant begins the medical screening, the process becomes a "black box," recruiters said, which makes dealing with applicant questions about their status extremely frustrating and problematic. This lack of transparency also led recruiters to perceive that accountability at MEPS sites is lacking, as applicants turn to recruiters rather than MEPS for answers about their medical processing status and outcomes. Some recruiters even mentioned a desire for more authority to disqualify applicants who have certain medical conditions that are more consistently problematic upfront—rather than send these applicants through medical screening—to save man-hours. However, these recruiters acknowledged that they do not have the medical training typically required for these decisions.

Army Medical Department Recruiting

We also spoke with representatives from AMEDD recruiting because officer candidates applying to be medical professionals in the Army do not use the DoDMERB system, but instead are medically processed through MEPS or MTFs. We asked AMEDD recruiting representatives about their experiences with officers receiving medical screenings at MEPS and any potential challenges with the process. AMEDD representatives echoed some of the same concerns as other stakeholders regarding travel time to get to a MEPS site if there is not one near the applicant, noted that customer service can be lacking, and also described the "assembly line" nature of MEPS. However, AMEDD representatives noted that at some MEPS, depending on the CMO's direction, "red carpet treatment" may be available to allow officer applicants to skip the long waits alongside enlisted applicants. AMEDD representatives said that MEPS processes are "tried and true," that MEPS are able to conduct most required medical tests on-site, and that the process is smooth. While AMEDD representatives recognized the location convenience of the DoDMERB system, they liked the "one-stop" medical testing at USMEPCOM.

DoDMERB "Customer" Perspectives

We reached out to admissions representatives from the service academies and ROTCs as "customers" of the DoDMERB system to understand their perspectives, identify any issues with the current process, and validate the concerns of other stakeholders. The participants we interviewed included representatives from each service academy admissions department and from ROTC programs from each of the services.

Challenges

Participants reported that one challenge with the current DoDMERB system is nondisclosure—both deliberate and unintended—of issues in applicants' medical histories. Nondisclosure often occurs with mental health conditions, they said, and parents sometimes influence applicants to not mention an issue (e.g., to downplay childhood mental health issues or hide a peanut allergy). Representatives stressed that nondisclosures make up just a handful of cases each year but can have major impacts. For ROTC cadets, for example, a nondisclosure can result in the service revoking an ROTC scholarship that a student was relying on to afford tuition. As discussed earlier, USMEPCOM representatives noted that private medical providers may be less likely to identify nondisclosed medical issues—a situation that seems to align with the experiences of the academy and ROTC stakeholders.

Representatives were also apprehensive about the quality of reports from civilian doctors, echoing concerns from USMEPCOM representatives that private medical providers may not understand the requirements of the military environment and may potentially advocate for applicants regardless.

In addition, representatives mentioned that some applicants have issues accessing private medical providers on contract with DoDMERB due to proximity or transportation limitations. This was particularly an issue among applicants in rural areas without access to transportation and in U.S. territories without a DoDMERB contracted medical provider nearby.

Academy and ROTC representatives noted challenges with the DoDMERB online systems. They expressed frustration with incompatible information technology systems that force them to load all medical files into each system. Representatives also indicated that different forms ask medical questions in different ways and interpreted this as a lack of standardization. However, OSD Accession Policy representatives noted that this is an intentional method used to trigger applicants to reveal nondisclosed issues that may be identified by certain questions and forms but not others.[18]

Despite the challenges raised by academy and ROTC stakeholders, these representatives expressed general satisfaction with DoDMERB and the current system and felt it was meeting their needs.

Views on Processing Candidates Through Military Entrance Processing Stations

We also asked representatives from the academies and ROTC about the feasibility of, and potential issues related to, processing officer applicants through MEPS rather than the current DoDMERB system. We sought to explore the concerns other stakeholders had raised about combining accession medical systems and to ensure that potential future systems are designed to meet the needs of the academies and ROTCs.[19]

Concerns about the enlisted culture at MEPS deterring elite officer applicants from pursuing military service did not resonate with most interview participants; it did to some degree with a few of the

---

[18] As will be discussed in the next chapter, AMWG is working on some of the standardization and information technology issues raised by stakeholders during our interviews.

[19] Note that the study did not receive qualitative data from USMEPCOM customers regarding any concerns related to potentially processing enlisted applicants through the DoDMERB system in the future. Thus, we are unable to provide a parallel comparison to DoDMERB customers' concerns about processing officer applicants through MEPS.

academies but not with any of the ROTC representatives. However, one related concern raised primarily by the academies was that enlisted recruiters could potentially "poach" officer applicants while at MEPS. Representatives from some academies thought that enlisted recruiters who frequent the MEPS could persuade officer applicants to enlist in a service in the near term rather than pursue the longer track of an officer career at an academy.

Some representatives from the academies and ROTC did echo concerns about the limited number of MEPS locations and increases in travel time serving as a deterrent to military service for officer applicants.

Overall, representatives had mixed feedback about whether processing officer applicants through MEPS would be an improvement over the current DoDMERB system. While they noted the increased travel time could be a deterrent for officer applicants, they also believed that using MEPS would likely improve the quality of exams. Despite some concerns, representatives from the academies and ROTC were generally open to participating in a potential future pilot program that involved their officer applicants using the USMEPCOM system if the pilot design considered their input and addressed their concerns to the extent possible.

Summary

USMEPCOM and DoDMERB both provide accession medical screening but use different business models and serve different (although slightly overlapping) applicant populations. USMEPCOM oversees 65 MEPS across the country that provide on-site medical exams and qualification determinations. Military recruiters and service liaisons play a central role, helping (mostly enlisted) applicants submit required medical paperwork in advance, taking applicants to MEPS locations, and acting as a go-between for the MEPS medical departments and a service's medical waiver authorities. In comparison, DoDMERB outsources most of the medical examination process to Concorde Inc., which supplies hundreds of medical providers across the country. Concorde also manages the scheduling of exams with applicants and providers. DoDMERB's role focuses on the actual medical qualification decision and coordinating with the officer accession sources and officer applicants about the results of their medical screening.

When asked about combining the two business models, USMEPCOM and DoDMERB stakeholders expressed concerns ranging from insufficient quality of examinations (USMEPCOM concern) to the inconvenience of officer applicants going to MEPS (DoDMERB concern). We also asked these systems' "customers"—that is, service academy admissions and ROTC admissions for DoDMERB and enlisted recruiters and AMEDD recruiting representatives for MEPS—about challenges they experience with the respective systems. These included a lack of consistency across MEPS (enlisted recruiter concern) and the uncertain quality of reports from civilian providers (officer accession sources' concern). DoDMERB customers expressed general satisfaction with DoDMERB, but many were also open to the idea of a potential future pilot study in which some of their officer applicants used the USMEPCOM system, as long as their input was taken into account during the planning phases. The study was not able to obtain information regarding MEPS customers' feedback on a future system that could send enlisted applicants through the DoDMERB system.

Based on our review of the two systems and the findings from DoDMERB and USMEPCOM stakeholders, we summarize the key advantages and disadvantages of each system relative to one another in Table 2.2. These advantages and disadvantages focus on several factors such as access, convenience, experience of medical examination staff, civilian versus military medical examination environment, consolidated functions, and capacity. This table does not include challenges that limit both systems, which are addressed in the next chapter.

In Chapter 3, we discuss ongoing efforts within DoD to improve accession medical processing and related accession system issues. We also discuss efforts in the recent past to pilot major reforms to the accession medical screening system.

Table 2.2
Relative Advantages and Disadvantages of the DoDMERB and
USMEPCOM Systems

	DoDMERB	USMEPCOM
Advantages	• Greater number of locations decreases travel time and cost requirements • Online scheduling convenience • Less potential for wait time at exams • Civilian medical exam environment is familiar to applicants	• Exams conducted by medical providers trained in and regularly exposed to accession medicine • Serves as a one-stop shop for numerous pre-accession functions for enlisted applicants • System designed to process large number of applicants
Disadvantages	• Private physicians have less exposure to accession medicine than those at MEPS • Serves only medical mission; applicants must go elsewhere for other pre-accession requirements • System currently designed for limited number of applicants	• Fewer locations result in increased travel time and cost • Lack of online scheduling convenience • Greater potential for wait time at exam • Military medical exam environment is unfamiliar to some applicants and may not be well received

Department of Defense and Service Efforts to Improve Accession Medical Screening Processes

This project is not the first to examine whether accession medical screening processes can be improved. Reform efforts have been made or attempted in the past and continue to this day. These efforts are outlined in this chapter. Our aim in reviewing past and current reform efforts was to identify what DoD and the services have tried (and are trying) to change about the systems, the types of challenges faced in making such changes, and how DoD might address such challenges if the goal is to reform the business models of the two systems.

Department of Defense's Ongoing Accession Process Reforms

We begin by reviewing ongoing efforts within DoD to reform accession processes, focusing on those that directly impact accession medical processing. This review briefly outlines key efforts and may not be comprehensive of all reform efforts within DoD.[1]

Department of Defense Working Groups

DoD has established executive steering committees and working groups to update and modernize military accessions policies, standards, and

---

[1] We relied on key stakeholders to provide information on past and ongoing reform efforts, as there is little to no information on these efforts in the public domain. We acknowledge that other reforms, particularly within the military services, may have been attempted over the years.

procedures, including medical screening processes. One group is the Medical and Personnel Executive Steering Committee's (MEDPERS's) AMWG. Per the committee's AMWG charter (MEDPERS, 2015):[2]

> The MEDPERS AMWG provides cross-functional leadership, guidance, and expertise to manage and vet issues related to Military Recruiting and Accession; helps to coordinate the need for and/or changes to business processes or policies; and, connects the existing and emerging information technology (IT) investments and initiatives supporting and/or impacting this business area.

The AMWG aims to resolve four main challenge areas in the accessions system, which were outlined in a 2015 white paper authored by P&R IM in DoD. Table 3.1 summarizes the four main challenge areas and solutions recommended by P&R IM.

According to SMEs who are involved with AMWG, AMWG has teams addressing the four challenge areas: (1) preparing for Military Health System (MHS) GENESIS, an electronic health record system for the entire MHS, including the accession medical system;[3] (2) advancing a proof-of-concept using verifiable medical information to examine medical qualification decisions at select MEPS sites;[4] (3) developing

---

[2]   Based on communication with an AMWG member in August 2018, the MEDPERS AMWG 2015 charter is being extended to allow completion of the original mandate.

[3]   In June 2016, Principal Deputy Assistant Secretary of Defense for Manpower and Reserve Affairs Stephanie Barna issued a memorandum requesting that accession organizations and working groups be included in the modernization efforts led by the Defense Healthcare Management Systems Modernization program. Although not stated in the memo, MHS GENESIS falls within the DHMSM program, according to USMEPCOM SMEs.

[4]   According to information provided by a USMEPCOM SME in 2016, the proof of concept was designed to use verifiable medical information (VMI) to determine if relevant medical information not disclosed by applicants who went through MEPS exists within VMI sources and to assess whether those applicants' medical qualifications would have changed had the VMI been available at the time they went through MEPS. In 2017, USMEPCOM signed a memorandum of agreement with DHA and with the Veterans Health Administration within the U.S. Department of Veterans Affairs to access the Joint Legacy Viewer (JLV), which provides VMI for individuals within DoD's health information systems. According to information provided by a USMEPCOM SME in March 2019, USMEPCOM HQ accessed

Table 3.1
Personnel and Readiness Information Management Findings and Recommendations to Modernize Accessions System

Challenge Areas	Recommended Solutions
1. Data collection and use relies too much on paper, is "resource-intensive"	Move toward an "electronic, standards-based" accession data system that all accession "partners" can use
2. Too much reliance on applicant "self-disclosure," which limits "comprehensive analysis and review" of applicant information to determine whether they meet standards	Allow for "comprehensive view and enhanced screening of all accession applicants" (e.g., collect biometrics on recruits; verify self-disclosed information from other validated data sources)
3. Officer appointment and enlistment policies and business processes are separate	"Develop and adopt common medical accessions policies and information requirements for all accessions"
4. Several fragmented systems for managing recruiting and accessions data along with limited coordination for costly initiatives aimed at reforming those systems	Improve coordination of data management system initiatives across recruitment and accession to maximize limited resources

SOURCE: P&R IM (2015).

common medical forms for the two systems; and (4) working on data standards to improve data management systems used for accessions processes.

AMWG also has a team working on a model for future accessions medicine. According to a USMEPCOM representative involved with the team, as of March 2019, the draft model, concept of operations, and integration guide have been submitted but have not yet been approved by AMWG.

JLV in 2018 to understand its capability and began a pilot effort with prior service applicants at eight MEPS in February 2019. A longer-term plan is to use JLV for all applicants going through MEPS. As with the MHS GENESIS effort, the pilot with JLV is being led by USMEPCOM but reported to AMWG.

According to information provided by a USMEPCOM SME in 2019, USMEPCOM is planning to fund a contract that would provide MEPS with information on applicants' medical prescriptions. The plan would be to pilot test the prescription-drug effort, with the goal of having both JLV and prescription information available for most MEPS applicants in FY 2020.

In addition to AMWG, the Defense Accession Data Systems Integration Working Group (DADSIWG), as chartered by the Deputy Assistant Secretary of Defense for Military Personnel Policy (DASD MPP), is "a forum for developing policy and procedures for enhancing the standardization, collection, and distribution of automated data and enlistment documentation in support of the accession process" (DoD Manual 1145.02, 2018, p. 50). DADSIWG includes representatives from the offices of DASD MPP, ASD for Manpower and Reserve Affairs, the military services, DoD Human Resources Activity, the Selective Service System, and USMEPCOM. Some members of AMWG are also members of DADSIWG.

Other working groups may also affect accession medical screening processes. A notable example is the Accession Medical Standards Working Group (AMSWG), which is "a forum for developing policy and procedures for medical accession standards" (DoD Manual 1145.02, 2018, p. 51). AMSWG can recommend changes to medical standards and to the types of examinations and screening practices that the two systems employ.[5] AMSWG convenes representatives from DoD and the services' medical and health offices (e.g., each service's surgeon general's office).

USMEPCOM's 2016 Strategic Plan and Medical Qualification Decisions

Besides working groups, USMEPCOM has published plans aimed at improving processes at MEPS locations. In 2016, USMEPCOM published a ten-year strategic plan that lists as its first goal the "improved flexibility, accuracy, consistency, and timeliness of medical qualification decisions" (USMEPCOM, 2016, p. 3). According to information provided by USMEPCOM SMEs to the project team in 2016, USMEPCOM planned to achieve this goal in three stages over the ten years. The first stage would implement MHS GENESIS, the electronic health record system, at the accession level over roughly a three-

---

[5]   DoD accession medical standards' policy, DoDI 6130.03, is approved by the Under Secretary of Defense for Personnel & Readiness. Therefore, changes to standards in the policy would need approval from leadership in DoD.

year period.[6] The second (three-year) stage would establish a medical prequalification capability at MEPS using the electronic health data. The third (four-year) stage would move USMEPCOM to a risk-based assessment of medical fitness instead of the current qualification/disqualification decision used at MEPS.

DoDMERB and USMEPCOM Efforts to Improve Data Management

As outlined in the previous discussion, DoD is moving toward an electronic health record system, MHS GENESIS, that will be employed at MEPS. However, DoDMERB and USMEPCOM are engaged in other efforts to manage and share medical data using IT solutions. Below, we briefly outline DoDMERB's and USMEPCOM's past challenges with IT reform as well as ongoing reform efforts, as provided through communications with DoDMERB and USMEPCOM SMEs in 2019.

DoDMERB

According to a DoDMERB SME, in 2007 the OSD comptroller approved replacement of DoDMERB's legacy data management system known as D2K. The Navy's Space and Naval Warfare Systems Command (SPAWAR) was selected to replace D2K with an upgraded system. However, the SPAWAR system ran into cost overruns and was later canceled. A letter from the Senate Subcommittee on Contracting and Financial Oversight in 2013 asked the Chief of Naval Operations at the time, ADM Jonathan Greenert, to brief the subcommittee to "discuss how it [SPAWAR] will address the DODMERB contract's cost overruns and the mediation requirements of the Interservice Support Agreement [for SPAWAR to provide software development for DoDMERB]" (McCaskill, 2013). According to the DoDMERB SME, SPAWAR contract support ended without a new system after having spent over $8 million.

---

[6] According to a USMEPCOM SME in 2019, funding was approved for MHS GENESIS use by USMEPCOM in June 2018. The work to configure MHS GENESIS for USMEPCOM use is expected to be completed in 2020 with a plan to pilot test the system at one or two MEPS. Although the MHS GENESIS work is being reported to AMWG, according to a USMEPCOM SME in 2019, USMEPCOM has oversight of this effort.

In 2017, DHA approved a new effort to improve DoDMERB's data management system. The new system, the Defense Medical Accessions Computing System (DMACS), was described in a 2018 factsheet published by DHA's Solution Delivery Division as having searchable databases, metrics data, streamlined "data communications" among key stakeholders (e.g., DoDMERB, applicants, contract providers, accession sources), and workflow automation for DoDMERB and contract medical personnel. According to the DoDMERB SME, as of early 2019, DMACS has not delivered on the capabilities outlined in the factsheet; instead, it has been unreliable for users and does not allow DoDMERB to capture and extract useful information. As a result, according to the SME, DoDMERB personnel, waiver review personnel, and others have reduced productivity as they navigate DMACS to complete their work.

USMEPCOM

In 2008, USMEPCOM contracted a vendor to replace USMIRS with the Virtual Interactive Processing System (VIPS). The goal of VIPS was to allow preprocessing activities to take place off-site, away from MEPS, to reduce processing time at MEPS. Then-USMEPCOM commander, COL Mariano Campos, anticipated that "with VIPS, the number of applicants and the days they spend in the MEPS will be cut in half. . . . With VIPS, it might be possible for an applicant to take an enlistment test, and complete medical pre-screening, background checks and waiver pre-screening without ever setting foot in a MEPS or a [Military Entrance Test] site" (2008, p. 3).

However, in 2012, OSD's Defense Logistics Agency reviewed the contract and determined that VIPS "failed to achieve a full deployment decision within five (5) years of when funds for program were first obligated" (Heimbaugh, 2012). VIPS was subsequently canceled as additional funds would have been required to complete the program.

As of winter 2019, USMEPCOM has been working on other IT reforms, including some that are relevant to medical processing activities. In one effort, USMEPCOM is working with DHA to access the Health Artifact and Image Management Solution (HAIMS) database. HAIMS is used by MHS to view and store medical records. The goal is for medical records collected at MEPS to be uploaded into HAIMS for access by the MHS instead of the current practice of having enlistees hand-carry sealed envelopes with their medical records from MEPS to their training bases. In addition to HAIMS access, USMIRS is being upgraded and replaced by the Defense Digital Service. Although it is not yet clear whether USMIRS will be replaced before MHS GENESIS comes online, USMIRS will be upgraded in the meantime to allow MEPS medical sections to upload medical information for services' access (e.g., for service waiver authority review).

Scope of Ongoing Reform Efforts

Although USMEPCOM and DoD working groups continue to seek solutions for updating and modernizing accession medical processes, ongoing efforts are not focused on fundamentally changing the two business models or the applicant populations whom they medically screen. Instead, ongoing efforts focus on identifying process efficiencies— including information-sharing and database management—and quality improvements within the existing USMEPCOM and DoDMERB business models.

Department of Defense's Past Reform Efforts

Since at least 1994, DoD has pursued multiple efforts to reform accession medical processes.[7] However, it was not until the mid-2000s

---

[7] In 1994, the Deputy Assistant Secretaries of Defense (Professional Affairs and Quality Assurance and Military Personnel Policy) commissioned a roughly $500,000 effort to design and develop a cost-effective, evidenced-based, and standardized medical examination to reduce redundancies between DoDMERB and USMEPCOM (Office of the Assistant Secretary of Defense [Health Affairs], 1994). The effort included a business process improvement analysis and a functional economic analysis. The business improvement analysis identified the need for a streamlined medical examination process and more coordination among key stakeholders to address medical accession challenges and help align medical research efforts. The functional economic analysis focused on two alternative medical screening/examination options and identified a third option (i.e., a combination of expanded medical history and modified medical exam) as yielding the highest probable savings and return on investment for DoD. The other two options were (1) conduct expanded medical history alone, and (2) conduct a comprehensive medical exam with medical history as was currently performed.

that DoD leaders directed USMEPCOM and DoDMERB to undertake pilot programs to evaluate ways to change the organizations or approaches used to deliver medical screening at accession. Our descriptions of these efforts are based on discussions with USMEPCOM and DoDMERB SMEs who have familiarity with them, as well as unpublished documentation (e.g., briefing slides) that they provided. We found limited publicly available information that documents these efforts, but we cite reports and policies where available.

In 2003, the Deputy Under Secretary of Defense, Military Personnel Policy (DUSD MPP) directed the USMEPCOM Commander to conduct a feasibility study concerning consolidating regional DoDMERB and USMEPCOM medical examination resources in West Virginia. The pilot would have allowed local enlisted applicants to get medical screening from DoDMERB's Concorde contractors in the state and a number of officer applicants to get medical screening from the MEPS in Beckley, West Virginia. Up to 1,000 physicals were to be executed over a six-month period. According to information provided by an SME, the West Virginia feasibility study was designed to assess whether a unified approach to medical screening would lead to cost savings and improved customer accessibility. This same SME indicated that a key problem for the effort was a change in leadership at USMEPCOM and slow initiation of the effort on the part of key stakeholders.

In 2005, DUSD MPP directed MEDPERS to assess the impact of having DoDMERB and USMEPCOM work together to share services for medical screening. This led to the 2006 Tennessee feasibility study, which was structured similarly to the West Virginia study. The Tennessee study's goals included identifying more cost-effective medical screening procedures; determining business practice improvements, such as reducing travel time for recruiters driving applicants to their appointments; determining steps needed to coordinate scheduling between the two systems; and reporting on customer benefits

---

According to SME input to the project team, the 1994 study yielded several reforms, but those reforms did not fundamentally change USMEPCOM's and DoDMERB's overall business models.

due to shared assets.[8] As with the earlier effort, the Tennessee study was ultimately canceled. According to an SME involved with this pilot effort, the key stakeholders had recommended ending the study due to low participation rates (42 exams completed by MEPS and two by DoDMERB). It is unclear why participation was so low, but SME discussions suggested that one key challenge involved problems scheduling applicants across the two systems (e.g., officer applicants in USMIRS).

Although the Tennessee study ended without meeting the expected participation levels, USMEPCOM conducted a cost analysis in 2006 to compare the cost of using USMEPCOM alone to screen all applicants with the cost of allowing USMEPCOM applicants to use either system.[9] Using the assumption of 5,635 medical exams per year, USMEPCOM estimated that screening applicants for both systems would cost $2.04 million. The cost of a system combining USMEPCOM and DoDMERB resources was estimated at $1.83 million—11 percent less (i.e., $216,520 in savings) than a USMEPCOM-only system. In part, savings could be realized because USMEPCOM medical examinations were slightly more expensive per person than DoDMERB exams ($187 versus $173). However, the cost analysis did not take into account that USMEPCOM covers applicant lodging and meal costs, while DoDMERB does not, and that enlisted applicants undergo additional types of medical assessments than officer applicants. Therefore, further examination would be needed to determine whether the cost comparisons account for all key differences in service delivery.

---

[8] Although the term "shared assets" is not defined in the briefing slides that we received about the Tennessee feasibility study, the context suggests that the term refers to resources being shared between USMEPCOM and DoDMERB in processing applicants for medical screening.

[9] Operationally, the costs were based on expenses directly paid by the government. Cost factors included those related to meals and lodging, pay for personnel directly involved in medical screening, fees for contract providers and consultants, and consultant transportation costs. (Information about this cost analysis is based on an unpublished 2006 USMEPCOM slide deck provided by an SME familiar with the Tennessee study.)

Service-Led Alternative Models for Accession Medical Screening Processes

In addition to DoD-directed efforts, the Army National Guard (ARNG), AMEDD, and the U.S. Marine Corps (USMC) Officer Candidate Course (OCC)/Platoon Leaders Class (PLC) accessions implemented alternatives to the MEPS-only accession medical screening their applicants would typically receive. We describe the 2008–2009 ARNG Hometown Physical Program and lessons from that program. We follow with a brief description of two related pilot efforts for AMEDD applicants and a description of the ongoing USMC OCC/PLC program, as well as challenges in evaluating its outcomes.

Army National Guard Hometown Physical Program

According to interviews with USMEPCOM SMEs in 2016, ARNG recruiting began a pilot program in 2008 modeled after DoDMERB. But instead of using contract providers to conduct medical screening, the program allowed private "hometown" providers (HTPs) to screen ARNG applicants. The USMEPCOM inspector general (IG) later examined the program, reviewing some cases of ARNG applicants separating from military training due to preexisting medical issues and interviewing medical personnel at MEPS, who observed that ARNG applicants go through MEPS for other accessions processes (e.g., oath of enlistments). The IG identified a number of problems with the program, most notably the questionable quality of medical examinations provided by several HTPs. The HTP program was discontinued in 2011.

In interviews, USMEPCOM SMEs cited this program as a cautionary tale for using the DoDMERB model to screen enlisted applicants. However, a key difference between the ARNG program and DoDMERB is that the ARNG program did not vet HTPs in advance, while DoDMERB requires its contractor to select and vet providers. Moreover, private HTPs might have an incentive to advocate for applicants instead of viewing their role as that of a medical provider who is screening for medical fitness to serve in the military. In effect, the incentive structure for private HTPs and vetted contract providers may be different. Unfortunately, we are not aware of an analysis that directly compares a private HTP program with DoDMERB's.

Army Medical Department Pilot Program

According to discussions with a small number of AMEDD representatives held in 2017, AMEDD piloted efforts to allow its medical professional applicants to receive accession medical screening through MEPS or MTFs, and later through MEPS, MTFs, or DoDMERB. An AMEDD representative involved with the pilot effort explained that the goal was to explore more options for AMEDD applicants' medical screening as the Army was ramping up forces after the September 11, 2001, attacks.[10] AMEDD teamed with Army Accessions Command and took 25 AMEDD applicants to Walter Reed Medical Center (an MTF) for their physicals. A majority (17 out of 25) indicated they liked receiving their medical exams at an MTF because they were able to meet with Army medical professionals (their peers) while on-site for their physicals. The AMEDD representative also noted that any specialty medical consultations could be done during the same MTF visit because many specialists work at the MTFs. By contrast, AMEDD applicants who are screened through MEPS and need specialty consultations would have to have those consultations done on a different day (since the specialists are not at MEPS) (U.S. Military Entrance Processing Command, 2006).

While conducting the pilot with the MTFs, DoDMERB offered to provide physicals to AMEDD applicants as well. This led to a second pilot effort in which an Army physician's assistant at USAREC screened applicants at MTFs, depending on physical health and age. Younger, healthier applicants were sent to MEPS for medical screening, while older, less healthy applicants went through DoDMERB. The AMEDD representative involved with the pilot effort noted that, while the DoDMERB system was convenient for the general physical exams,

---

[10] As with other pilot efforts, the information provided to RAND about the AMEDD pilot efforts are limited to discussions with a small number of SMEs. These individuals have first-hand knowledge of the pilot efforts because they had some involvement with them at the time. However, we caution the reader that others who were involved with these efforts may have additional information or perspectives that are not included here.

applicants had to go back into the Concorde system to schedule any required specialty consultations and associated medical tests. If there were delays with scheduling specialty consultation through Concorde, applicants would have to arrange for consultations with providers outside the DoDMERB system and pay the associated costs. Also, results from the tests would have to be reviewed by the USAREC surgeon. As a result of these challenges, AMEDD returned to using MEPS and MTFs for their applicants.

U.S. Marine Corps Officer Candidate Course/Platoon Leaders Class Program

In 2010, USMC implemented a nationwide program that allows its OCC/PLC applicants to be screened at either DoDMERB sites or at USMEPCOM locations (where OCC/PLC applicants had typically gone in the past). Between 2010 and 2014, the Marine Corps accession pilot processed over 4,100 people. Marine Corps leadership claimed that the program provided applicants more convenient options for medical screening than a MEPS-only process. It also saved money for the Department of the Navy (of which the Marine Corps is part) because the Navy's Bureau of Medicine and Surgery did not have to provide the final qualification decision for applicants, which was provided by DoDMERB instead (Milstead, 2014). Because the program began as an informal agreement between the Marine Corps and DoDMERB, the Marine Corps asked that DoD formalize the program. DoD approved the request in 2014, stipulating that Marine Corps recruiters send applicants who live within 50 miles of a MEPS site to the MEPS site instead of a DoDMERB location (Arendt, 2014), and the pilot is still ongoing.

At first glance, it would appear that the USMC pilot program should provide generalizable evidence for policymakers on creating a hybrid model for the two accession medical screening systems. We attempted to explore this option by requesting data from USMC, DoDMERB, and USMEPCOM. Table 3.2 provides the list of data elements we requested at the individual applicant level. We group these elements into four main categories for analysis: processing times, proximity to exam locations, medical qualification decisions about the

Table 3.2
Data Elements Requested to Evaluate USMC OCC/PLC Program

Category	Data Elements

Processing times	• Application year or date
	• Date that medical accessions process was initiated (e.g., date that applicant entered Concorde system to request an appointment; date that MEPS was first notified that applicant would require medical examination)
	• Date(s) for critical decision points in process:
	  o Initial medical exam(s)
	  o Waiver request sent to waiver authority (if applicable)
	  o Specialist consult(s) (if applicable)
	  o Waiver approved (if applicable)
	  o Medical qualification decision made and/or applicant notified of decision

Proximity to exam locations	• Applicant zip code • Applicant accession source • Concorde location(s) or MEPS location where applicant received exam(s)
Medical qualification decisions	• Waiver decision, if applicable (e.g., approved vs. not approved) • Medical qualification decision (e.g., approved vs. not approved)
Accession decision	• If applicant ultimately accessed (if available)
Other information	• Whether applicant is prior enlisted (if available)

applicants, and applicant acceptance into OCC/PLC. We also asked about applicants' prior enlistment (in the category of "Other information") to determine what proportion of applicants would have been previously exposed to military exam environments (while enlisted) and to assess potential differences of those applicants from those without that exposure.

However, we discovered that the USMC program does not provide useful information for policymakers for several reasons. First, no systematic data were collected from applicants. USMC, DoDMERB, and USMEPCOM could provide our team only with aggregate numbers associated with the program, citing challenges with data systems or not having all of the data at the individual level. To assess the impact on outcomes and outputs of the screening systems, individual-level information about the program participants is needed. More important, even if we were able to acquire individual-level data about the participants, it is not clear that we would have been able to measure outputs and outcomes of the systems after the fact. For example, participants' experience while going through the screening processes would be difficult to retrospectively measure because memories about the processes may have faded since they went through them.

Second, and most important, the design of the USMC pilot program cannot produce generalizable evidence about the causal impact of the combined medical screening system for a methodological reason—namely, that the OCC/PLC applicants who used MEPS are not a representative sample of the applicants who will be processed in a combined medical screening system. OCC/PLC applicants may differ from other officer applicants, most of whom apply for ROTC and the military academies, and from enlisted applicants across the military services.

Finally, the OCC/PLC participants who choose either MEPS or a DoDMERB medical provider can be systematically different in ways that we may not be able to fully capture by analysis of observable characteristics (e.g., age of participants). Characteristics we do not observe (e.g., preferences for the method by which the medical exams are scheduled) might be correlated with the outputs and outcomes that we want to measure, which would hinder interpretation of the relationship between the observable characteristics and the outputs and outcomes. Under these conditions, we cannot draw a valid inference about the impact of a hybrid accession medical screening process using the information from the USMC OCC/PLC program.

Summary

Over time, DoD has sought ways to improve how it processes applicants for medical fitness. Ongoing efforts primarily involve working groups of key stakeholders (including DoDMERB and USMEPCOM representatives) to standardize and streamline efforts, as well as modernize data standards and management systems. However, ongoing efforts are not aimed at the fundamental business models of either system. In the mid-2000s, DoD leaders did commission efforts in two states to examine how a hybrid system allowing applicants to choose either DoDMERB or MEPS for screening would affect costs and applicants' "customer" experiences, among other outcomes. These efforts "failed to launch," however, and so they were unable to fully answer the basic question of whether a hybrid medical screening system could provide greater efficiencies and higher-quality outcomes than two separate systems.

An alternative approach to medical screening used by ARNG in its 2008–2009 HTP program also ended after the USMEPCOM IG cited quality concerns with the program. In addition, while AMEDD attempted to provide medical professionals accessing into the Army the option of MEPS, MTFs, or DoDMERB exam locations in the early to mid-2000s, it ran into challenges for their unique population of medical professionals. Although ARNG and AMEDD did not succeed in retaining their pilot programs, a 2010 program established by the USMC for OCC/PLC applicants to use either DoDMERB or MEPS remains in place.

There are limitations in using previous and existing programs that combine MEPS and the DoDMERB contractors to infer the impact of potential reform efforts on outputs and outcomes of an accession medical screening system. For instance, the USMC program lacks systematic applicant data that can be analyzed to evaluate system outcomes, and even if it had such data, the results of an analysis of the program cannot be generalized to other applicant populations. Expanding the program to other applicant populations can address the generalizability limitation, but there would remain the limitation of selection bias (i.e., systematic differences in the way applicants choose which system to use). As we discuss in Chapters 5 and 6, systematic data collection and randomized control trials (RCTs) in pilot programs could address these limitations.

In the next chapter, we take a step back from discussing pilot and reform programs and outline three COAs to change the business models behind accession medical screening systems and the potential implications of adopting each COA. We also identify which of the three COAs may present the least risk to DoD and should therefore be selected for adoption. We then follow with a chapter on design elements for a pilot program(s) to evaluate the selected COA's outcomes.

CHAPTER FOUR

Courses of Action for Business Model Changes to Accession Medical Screening Systems

Previous attempts at piloting changes to the business models used for accession medical screening processes have generally focused on a hybrid system in which officer and enlisted applicants can go through either DoDMERB or MEPS for medical screening. However, a hybrid system is just one of three possible changes to the business model. In this chapter, we outline three COAs that DoD could consider for changing the business models for accession medical screening systems and assess the potential impacts of implementing each one.

Courses of Action on a Continuum of Outsourcing Medical Screening

The three main COAs we present reflect three levels on a continuum of outsourcing medical screening to contract providers at nongovernment facilities. We developed this framing based on our review of the two business models and our finding that the key difference between them is the level of outsourcing. DoDMERB's business model represents a high degree of outsourcing (COA 1, "High Outsource"), while the USMEPCOM model represents a low degree of outsourcing (COA 2, "Low Outsource"). Between these two levels is a moderate degree of outsourcing, or a hybrid of the two models (COA 3, "Hybrid").

We also identified several variations for COAs 1 and 3. COA 1 has two variations:

a. DoDMERB only: DoDMERB processes all accession medical screening
b. USMEPCOM contract: USMEPCOM contracts with external health care providers to perform medical screening at nongovernmental facilities (i.e., no more medical screening at MEPS), as DoDMERB continues to do the same.

The variations for COA 3 reflect three points on a continuum, from giving applicants little to no choice to giving them high levels of choice of where to receive medical examinations.

a. No choice: DoD and the services determine which of the two systems applicants use
b. Reduced choice: Applicants and/or recruiters can choose medical screening location(s) within certain parameters set by DoD (e.g., USMC OCC/PLC model where applicants go to MEPS if within 50 miles; otherwise, they can go to DoDMERB)
c. Full choice: Applicants and/or recruiters can choose to go to MEPS or through DoDMERB for medical screening with no constraints set by DoD.

To summarize, COA 1 reflects the DoDMERB business model in which applicants receive medical screening by nongovernmental providers at off-site locations. COA 2 presents the USMEPCOM model in which medical screening can occur only at government facilities, namely, MEPS.[1] COA 3 is a hybrid of the two, allowing applicants to use either system, although DoD can limit the choice.[2]

---

[1] MTFs are also government facilities and could be part of COA 2. However, we do not discuss the role of MTFs given that the focus is on the two main business models used by USMEPCOM and DoDMERB.

[2] While COA 3 could involve a single system run by DoDMERB alone, USMEPCOM alone, or one organization working for the other (e.g., DoDMERB subsumed under USMEPCOM), we do not explicitly discuss such a system. As outlined in the next section, the hybrid model has unclear implications for system capacity. Including a single-organization version of the hybrid model would add complexity on top of this uncertainty.

Potential Impact of Each Course of Action on DoDMERB and USMEPCOM

The business models used by DoDMERB and USMEPCOM directly affect how DoDMERB and USMEPCOM organize and structure their resources and activities to deliver the desired outputs and outcomes, and how they apply different levels of resources to execute their accession medical missions. Therefore, we assess the potential impact of each COA on DoDMERB and USMEPCOM.

For the assessment, we developed three criteria based on key differences between the current systems (e.g., large enlisted applicant population served by MEPS compared to smaller officer applicant population served by DoDMERB), as well as themes from prior reform efforts (e.g., challenges in communication when leadership changes or when trying to send applicants to a different system) and ongoing reform efforts (e.g., move toward electronic health record systems for more complete and secure information-sharing), which were described in the previous chapters. Specifically, we identified organization, capacity, and information-sharing as criteria.

Organization refers to how DoDMERB and USMEPCOM structure their resources and activities for the accession medical mission. Organization as we define it covers many of the factors involved in the U.S. military's Doctrine, Organization, Training, Materiel, Leadership/Education, Personnel, Facilities, and Policy (DOTMLPF-P) framework.[3] *Capacity* refers to level of resources required for each system to execute the accession medical screening mission. We selected this criterion because of the large difference in the sizes of the enlisted

---

[3] DOTMLPF-P framework is used in defense acquisition planning to determine whether military missions can be executed satisfactorily with current DOTMLPF-P and, if not, what capabilities are needed to fill gaps. *Doctrine* concerns the guidance and operating procedures for how to execute the missions; *organization* refers to how people, equipment, and activities are structured for the missions; *training* focuses on how personnel are prepared for the missions; *materiel* covers equipment and systems needed for the missions; *leadership/education* refers to how military leaders are developed and prepared to lead the missions; *personnel* focuses on availability of qualified individuals and units to perform the missions; *facilities* covers the government property needed for the missions; and *policy* is focused on whether policy allows for successful implementation of the other DOTMLPF areas. See Manning (2019) for more details on DOTMLPF-P in defense acquisition planning.

applicant population (which USMEPCOM currently serves) and the officer applicant population (which DoDMERB currently serves). *Information sharing* reflects the idea that each COA has different requirements for key stakeholder involvement and thus different communication levels and needs (which past reform efforts suggest can be a challenge to address).

We apply the three criterion categories to each COA variation to assess potential impacts on DoDMERB and USMEPCOM systems.[4] We define relative levels of expected impact for the three criterion categories in Table 4.1.[5]

Table 4.1
Criteria for Assessing Potential Impacts of Courses of Action on DoDMERB and USMEPCOM Accession Medical Screening Systems

Criterion Category	Expected Level of Impact on System from Adopting COA		
	Major	Minor	None
Organization	Significant change (loss or gain) in structure of resources (e.g., personnel) and medical screening processing activities	Limited change in structure of resources and activities	No change in structure of resources or activities
Capacity	Significant change in size of population served	Limited change in size of population served	No change in size of population served
Information Sharing	Formal communication/data-sharing channels needed for more than one category of stakeholders (options include: enlisted accession sources and waiver authorities, officer accession sources and waiver authorities, applicants/recruiters, contract provider firms [e.g., Concorde])	Formal communication/data-sharing channels needed for one additional category of stakeholders	No additional communication/data-sharing channels

---

[4]   We do not estimate financial costs associated with the COAs, as we did not have sufficient information about specific cost factors for USMEPCOM and DoDMERB, although we would imagine that financial costs would vary by COA. See Chapter 2 for a discussion about challenges in comparing DoDMERB and USMEPCOM.

[5]   We used three levels for expected impact because military planners typically describe risk using three levels of low, medium, and high. We do not conduct a formal risk analysis

In addition to the three relative levels of expected impact in Table 4.1, we also use two other codes: nonapplicable and unclear. Non-applicable code is used when the criterion (e.g., capacity) does not apply for the given organization (i.e., DoDMERB or USMEPCOM) for the given COA variation (e.g., COA 1a). The "unclear" code is used when the potential outcomes can vary so widely that we could not assess the potential impact.

We summarize our impact assessments in two figures, one for DoDMERB (Figure 4.1) and another for USMEPCOM (Figure 4.2).

Figure 4.1
Potential Impact of Courses of Action on DoDMERB Accession Medical System

COA Variations	Organization	Capacity	Information Sharing
COA 1. High Outsource Model			
1a. DoDMERB only	May need additional HQ section(s)	Large influx of enlisted applicants	Add multiple new communication channels
1b. USMEPCOM contract	Continues with current model	Continues serving current population	Communicates with current stakeholders
COA 2. Low Outsource Model			
2. MEPS only	DoDMERB would not be needed	Not applicable	Not applicable
COA 3. Hybrid Model			
3a. No choice	May need additional HQ section(s)	DoD/services can balance applicant flows across systems	Add multiple new communication channels
3b–c. Reduced or full choice	Same as above	Unclear; depends on applicant flows	Same as above

Key: Potential impact
■ Major   ■ Minor   ■ None   ■ Unclear   ■ Not applicable

because we do not have data to estimate probabilities that DoDMERB or MEPS would not be able to complete their missions under each COA variation. (See Gerstein et al. [2016] for a detailed description of risk assessment methodologies.) However, COA features with higher levels of expected impact may be riskier than features with lower levels of expected impact in terms of disrupting current DoDMERB and MEPS operations.

Figure 4.2
Potential Impact of Courses of Action on USMEPCOM Accession Medical System

COA Variations	Organization	Capacity	Information Sharing
COA 1. High Outsource Model			
1a. DoDMERB only	MEPS medical section has minimal activity	Not applicable	Not applicable
1b. USMEPCOM contract	Same as above	Continues serving current population	Add communications with contract provider firm
COA 2. Low Outsource Model			
2. MEPS only	HQ liaison with officer applicants	Add small officer applicant population	Add communications with officer accession sources
COA 3. Hybrid Model			
3a. No choice	HQ liaison with officer applicants	DoD/services can balance applicant flows across systems	Add multiple new communication channels
3b–c. Reduced or full choice	Same as above	Unclear; depends on applicant flows	Same as above

Key: Potential impact
■ Major ■ Minor ■ None ■ Unclear ■ Not applicable

In each figure, we code our assessments based on expected impact compared to the baseline of each organization's current system.

For DoDMERB, all COAs have at least one major impact, with differences depending on COA variation. For COA 1a, the high outsource model, DoDMERB may experience some minor changes to its HQ to add sections that could process the influx of medical exam packages from enlisted applicants, but we would not expect other major changes in the organizational structure of DoDMERB activities. We do expect a major impact in terms of capacity because of the large number of enlisted applicants. For a sense of scale, DoDMERB handles about 30,000 officer applicants a year. An additional 300,000 applicants from the enlisted side would be a 1,000-percent increase in applicant load for DoDMERB. In terms of information sharing, DoDMERB would need to add formal communication channels with multiple sources on the enlisted accession side (enlisted applicants, recruiters, recruiting commands, training commands), while maintaining communication/information flows with officer accession sources, officer applicants, Concorde, and DoD entities (e.g., DHA).

For COA 1b, in which USMEPCOM contracts its own off-site services, DoDMERB would not experience changes, as it would continue operations with its current population.

For COA 2, where MEPS medical sections handle all military applicants' medical screening, DoDMERB would not be needed as an organization for accession medical screening. This means that capacity and information sharing are not applicable if DoDMERB as an organization is removed from the accession medical screening mission.

For COA 3, we expect both minor and major changes regardless of the variation of the COA. Minor changes are expected in terms of organization to handle enlisted applicants (akin to organizational changes for COA 1a). However, capacity changes will depend on how many enlisted applicants go to DoDMERB and how many officer applicants who would otherwise have gone through DoDMERB would now go to USMEPCOM for medical screening. In the no-choice version of COA 3 (COA 3a), DoD and the services could control which system applicants use in a way that would limit major fluctuations in DoDMERB's applicant flow. DoDMERB should therefore not have major changes in capacity under this variation of the COA. However, for the variations in which applicants or their recruiters have more choice of where to go (COA 3b–c), the impact on DoDMERB capacity is unclear. It could range from having little to no change to having major impact. Regardless of the COA 3 variation, we expect a major impact on DoDMERB's information-sharing requirements akin to COA 1a.

Like DoDMERB, USMEPCOM would face a range of potential impacts depending on the COA. For COA 1a, the largest impact to USMEPCOM would be reduced functionality at the MEPS medical sections since the medical exam activity would occur offsite with contractors (either through DoDMERB's contract in COA 1a or USMEPCOM's contract in COA 1b). However, USMEPCOM would not be expected to experience major impacts for COA 1b in terms of capacity: MEPS medical sections would still need to conduct some minimal processing of the enlisted applicants even if exams are conducted off-site, and oversight functions would still be needed at USMEPCOM HQ. For COA 1a, information-sharing requirements would somewhat increase for USMEPCOM, as it would involve coordinating with a contract provider that is offering off-site services.

In COA 2, MEPS medical sections would have to increase capacity to account for the extra 30,000 officer applicants, but that is a small increase relative to the current population that the MEPS system collectively serves. USMPECOM may need to add some kind of liaison for officer applicants, akin to how DoDMERB communicates directly with officer applicants on their qualification outcomes. USMEPCOM would also need to add a communication channel with additional officer accession sources (e.g., the service academies).

COA 3 impacts are expected to follow the same patterns for USMEPCOM as they do for DoDMERB. The organizational structure would not change significantly, but multiway communications would be needed for any hybrid system in which enlisted applicants and officer applicants can go to either system.

Selecting a Course of Action

The three COAs represent significant shifts in how DoDMERB and USMEPCOM do business when it comes to accession medical screening processing. COA 1 would reduce the role of MEPS medical sections while also potentially increasing the capacity and information-sharing requirements of DoDMERB. COA 2 would all but remove DoDMERB from the accession medical screening business while MEPS would have to contend with a somewhat larger applicant pool and communicate with additional stakeholders on the officer applicant side. Finally, a hybrid model would require DoDMERB and USMEPCOM to communicate with several parties and potentially contend with unpredictable applicant flows, particularly if applicants were given full choice of which of the two medical screening systems to use.

If DoD were to choose one COA based on the potential impacts outlined above, as well as the relative advantages and disadvantages outlined in Table 2.2, COA 3 may present the least risk among the three COAs, because it would not involve a significant divestment of either organization's structure and staff (although it is important to note that maintaining the infrastructure and staffing levels of both organizations has the potential to be less efficient than focusing resources on just one organization, as with COAs 1 and 2). Also, COA 3 does not remove all of the relative advantages of one system. For example, as Table 2.2 shows, DoDMERB has a relative advantage over the USMPECOM system in terms of a larger number of exam locations, which can provide greater geographic flexibility/convenience to applicants and recruiters. Under COA 2, that advantage would be lost because the COA assumes all applicants would go to MEPS. Under COA 1 the MEPS' "one-stop shop" processing for enlisted personnel who would get medical examinations off-site while also going to MEPS for nonmedical processing would be lost.

COA 3 also has the advantage over the other two COAs in that it allows DoD to determine how well applicants from each system would fare in the other system. Moreover, DoD has a model for a hybrid system in the USMC OCC/PLC program. Adopting COA 3 could involve an expansion of this program to other accession sources, particularly if the USMC OCC/PLC program demonstrates positive aspects (e.g., lower costs) that provide insights into features to consider when expanding a hybrid model to other accession sources.

Summary

We proposed three COAs for changing the business models used for accession medical screening systems. The COAs represent a continuum from a high level of outsourcing of medical examination (COA 1) to a lower level of outsourcing (COA 2), with a hybrid of insourcing and outsourcing as a third option (COA 3). COAs 1 and 3 have variations that would affect DoDMERB and USMEPCOM in different ways.

We also provided an assessment of the potential impact of each COA on DoDMERB's and USMEPCOM's current business models. We compared each COA against three criterion categories: organization, capacity, and information sharing. Clearly, COAs that would significantly reduce the functionality of DoDMERB (COA 2) or USMEPCOM (COA 1a) have the greatest potential impact on the organizations. Barring those extreme cases, the hybrid model (COA 3) has the greatest potential impact on both DoDMERB and USMEPCOM in terms of information-sharing requirements because a hybrid requires both organizations to communicate with multiple officer and enlisted accession stakeholders as well as with applicants. Under variations of COA 3 that give applicants more choice, predicting applicant flow for each system would be a challenge.

Although there are uncertainties with a hybrid model under COA 3, we expect it would present lower risk overall than COAs 1 and 2. Unlike COAs 1 and 2, COA 3 does not assume significant changes to either organization's structure and staff, and would not remove relative advantages of one system over the other. It does allow applicants from each system to go to the other system (cross-flows), and the USMC OCC/PLC program provides an existing template on which to build a larger hybrid model.

Before fully implementing COA 3, fundamental questions about each system's effectiveness and efficiency may need to be answered first. To help DoD address these questions, we outline in the next chapter how DoD can design a pilot program to examine key outcomes of a hybrid system.

CHAPTER FIVE

Designing Pilot Programs to Assess Course of Action Outcomes

At the end of the last chapter, we indicated that a hybrid model for an accession medical screening system may be a less risky COA than COAs that involve adopting one model over another. We also noted that the USMC OCC/PLC program could serve as a template for a hybrid model. However, as we described in Chapter 3, the USMC OCC/PLC program has not been evaluated to address fundamental questions about differences between the two current systems in terms of the consistency and accuracy of qualification decisions, efficiency (e.g., costs, timeliness), and stakeholder (e.g., applicant) experiences. Pilot programs would allow DoD to determine if the USMC OCC/ PLC program could be expanded to other accession sources to create a fully hybrid model for accessions medical screening processes.

In this chapter, we describe the design of a pilot program for a hybrid model that is based on an RCT. A key benefit of an RCT is that it involves randomly assigning participants to experimental conditions, meaning that it controls for potential systematic differences in the way applicants would choose which system to go to for medical screening processing. A well-designed RCT would also involve controls for systematic differences in characteristics of the MEPS and DoDMERB (via Concorde) contract locations. As such, RCTs represent a "gold standard" for testing differences between systems.

The chapter follows a three-step process for pilot program design:

1. Determine and develop the measurements for outputs and outcomes that are specified in the logic model and are of particular interest to policymakers.
2. Compute the minimum number of applicants who will be able to detect the impact of competing options, based on the distributions of the measurements and input from the decisionmakers.
3. Strategically select experimental sites and randomly assign applicants to MEPS locations or DoDMERB contractors.

These three steps were informed by guidance on program evaluation (e.g., GAO, 2012), although details about specific features (measures, sample sizes, sites, and so on) were derived from our own reviews and analyses. Following the description of an RCT for a hybrid model, we conclude with a brief outline of the factors that would affect costs of designing and executing this kind of pilot program.

Step 1: Determine and Develop Measures for Desired Outputs and Outcomes

A pilot program can be designed within a program evaluation framework, as we discussed briefly in Chapter 1. The typical starting point for program evaluation is developing a logic model of the program (or system) to be evaluated. A logic model is a systematic depiction of how a program (or a process) functions to achieve the desired outputs and outcomes (GAO, 2012, p. 10). "A program logic model links outcomes (both short- and long-term) with program activities/processes and the theoretical assumptions/principles of the program" (W. K. Kellogg Foundation, 2004, p. 3). Logic models are helpful for encouraging decisionmakers to consider the full range of factors that affect outcomes of interest. Definitions and examples of the main components of a logic model are outlined in Table 5.1.

In the next section, we describe how we used a design workshop with key stakeholder groups of accession medical screening systems to solicit their insights into desired outcomes, outputs, and measures for an accession medical screening system (regardless of its form). We also

Table 5.1
Definitions of Logic Model Components

Component	Definition	Examples
Context	Environmental factors that affect system design and implementation	• National security strategy • U.S. employment rates • Military service force structures
Inputs	Resources and policy that affect the design, development, and maintenance of the system	• Personnel who conduct medical screening • Data management systems for applicant data • Medical exam facilities • DoD medical standards policy
Activities	Design, development, and implementation of the system	• Recruiter driving time to get recruits to MEPS • Medical qualification decisions • Transmission of applicant health information to waiver reviewers
Outputs	Direct and immediate products of inputs and activities	• Number of applicants who are medically screened • Type and level of qualification decisions made • Recruiter and applicant reactions to treatment during screening process
Outcomes	Longer-term effects of the system	• Medical fitness for military service • Timeliness • Experience of care
Evaluation	Methods and data sources used to address questions about the efficiency and effectiveness of the system	• Manpower analyses to determine personnel needs • Analysis of training attrition from screening errors • Pilot programs to test different aspects of system changes

SOURCES: Definitions adapted from descriptions in GAO (2012); McLaughlin and Jordan (1999); Taylor-Powell and Henert (2008); and W. K. Kellogg Foundation (2004).

gathered information about inputs for a pilot program, which were part of a demonstration of a GIS interactive tool we developed.

Because we want to limit technical details that would not appeal to a broad policy audience, we created additional appendices that provide methodological and technical details about the design workshop (Appendix B) and how we developed the logic model (Appendix C).

Design Workshop for Exploring Key Parameters of a Pilot Program

In September 2017, we hosted 23 SMEs representing key stakeholders of the accession medical systems—OUSD/P&R/MPP (AP), DHA, DoDMERB, USMEPCOM, service representatives, and service waiver review authorities. We had three objectives: determine key strategic elements of a pilot program, shape a site selection procedure for the pilot program, and explore methodological considerations (particularly, site selection) using a GIS interactive tool.[1]

We facilitated the participants' discussions using the key components of a logic model. During the workshop, we asked participants to first identify what should be included as outcomes of an accession medical screening system (regardless of its form). We then asked them to provide ideas for the types of outputs they would expect from the system. We followed with a demonstration of the GIS interactive tool, which integrates data about applicant locations and medical exam locations, among other information about MEPS production (e.g., number of medical exams given annually) and provides analytic capabilities to help decisionmakers select geographic locations for a pilot study.[2] As part of that demonstration, we asked participants to describe inputs for the system, although they supplemented these inputs with those for selecting locations for a pilot study.

During discussions of these three components, participants commented on other components of the logic model. They specified environmental factors and key inputs that would shape a pilot program combining the two accession medical screening processes into one system, policy changes that would be needed, activities related to implementing the pilot program, and the program's desired outputs and outcomes.

In Table 5.2, we provide a short summary of factors that workshop participants suggested for an accession medical screening process-

---

[1] Although a focus of the pilot program discussion at the workshop was to send officer applicants to MEPS or DoDMERB contractors to compare outcomes across the two systems, the design principles we describe can be applied to other pilot programs such as a hybrid that sends officer applicants and enlisted applicants to different systems.

[2] We describe the GIS interactive tool in more detail in step 3, with technical details in appendices.

Table 5.2
Summary of Recommended Factors for Sample Pilot from Design Workshop

Logic Model Component	Recommended Types of Factors
Context	• Availability of new technologies to improve medical decision-making (e.g., artificial intelligence) • Represent all of the services (as they have different manning requirements tied to their missions, structure, etc.)
Inputs[a]	• Size of MEPS • Characteristics of applicants who use the location • Demographics of the local area • Efficiency of MEPS • Average driving time
Activities	• Test use of electronic health record system to transmit information among medical experts (e.g., MEPS CMO sends medical documents directly to service medical waiver authority)
Outputs	• Throughput (numbers and types of applicants processed, type and number of qualification decisions, costs and time to complete the process) • Stakeholders' reactions (applicant knowledge of, and experiences with, processes, experiences of representatives from services)
Outcomes	• Provides a high-quality product to the services (e.g., evidence-based decisions, consistent application of standards, sufficient information for service waiver decisions) • Directly supports continuity of care in the Military Health System • Promotes force readiness • Applicants have a positive experience of care, and system has sufficient transparency for stakeholders • Timely and lower cost (i.e., efficient) system
Evaluation	• Random assignment of pilot participants to conditions • Use civilian health exchange data to verify medical history information provided by applicants

NOTE: [a] For inputs, workshop participants focused on inputs for selecting locations for a pilot study, not inputs to a system.

ing system. We do not include all factors described by participants as some focus on implementation considerations for a pilot effort (e.g., getting support from commanders of MEPS where a pilot program would take place). See Appendix B for more information on the workshop agenda and approach for reviewing the workshop participants' recommendations.

We developed a detailed logic model based on our review of current accession medical screening processes (including discussions with stakeholders) but supplemented with workshop inputs as described in Table 5.2. The detailed logic model is shown in Figure 5.1.[3]

Measures and Metrics for a Pilot Program

The success of the system comes down to the achievement of desired outcomes. As shown in the logic model (Figure 5.1), we identified three categories of outcomes: (1) effectiveness (i.e., whether the system produces the intended outcomes), (2) efficiency (i.e., the least amount of resources were expended to achieve each desired outcome), and (3) experience (i.e., customer satisfaction, or how well key stakeholders such as applicants, recruiters, and accession sources believe the system meets their needs). For example, in Figure 5.1, medical fitness to serve (readiness) is considered an outcome geared toward effectiveness: Did the medical screening system accurately screen who would be medically fit for service and who would not? By way of comparison, the outcome of timeliness is focused on efficiency: Did the system produce the effectiveness-oriented outcomes (e.g., medical fitness) in the least amount of time possible for key stakeholders (including applicants) to move forward with the accession process?

Although program (or system) success is ultimately about achieving desired outcomes, outcomes can be difficult to measure because they are naturally long-term features and consequences of the system. For example, evaluating the outcome of medical fitness to serve includes (1) considerations of the ability of service members to be free of medical conditions, defects, or diseases that could harm themselves and others; as well as (2) assessment of service members' medical fitness to complete military education and training and perform the duties of their military occupations. Medical fitness to serve also means members are able to deploy to various geographical locations.[4] Assessing the

---

[3]   To keep the discussion of the pilot program design streamlined, we do not go into detail about the development and features of the logic model here. See Appendix C for a description of the detailed logic model.

[4]   DoDI 6103.03 (2018, p. 4) outlines health, performance, and readiness goals for medical screening, which include accessions medical screening. The key readiness goal describes

Figure 5.1
Logic Model for an Accession Medical Screening System

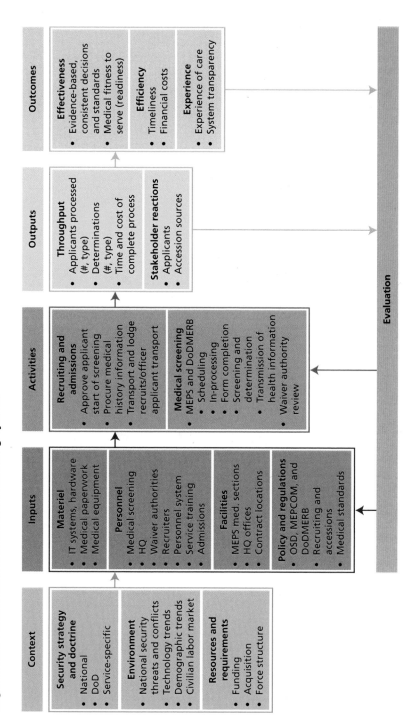

medical fitness outcome, therefore, requires years of data collection, particularly for many officer applicants who spend years preparing in academies and ROTC programs to become commissioned officers.

Many pilot programs focus on outputs because they are more direct and immediate products of the system. A pilot program interested in this outcome might first measure an output of the levels and types of medical qualification decisions that have been made in one year.

Because of the challenges of measuring outcomes, we recommend both nearer-term outcomes as well as output measures and metrics for each category of outcome of an RCT of a hybrid system.[5] Table 5.3 briefly lists the measures and metrics.

Table 5.3
Recommended Measures and Metrics for Pilot Program

Outcome Category	Measures and Metrics
Effectiveness	Accuracy: proportion of participants who separate from enlisted (basic and initial skills) training or from officer accession source due to EPTS medical reasons
	Reliability: audit of medical information used to make qualification decisions
Efficiency	Timeliness: length of applicant processing time, average commuting times to exam sites
	Financial costs: medical screening costs per applicant
	Time and cost: number and types of steps or phases in process
Experience	Surveys, interviews, and/or focus groups with participants, recruiters, and accession sources

NOTE: Measures and metrics are based on authors' reviews of the current systems, past and current reforms, as well as being informed by program evaluation guidance from literature (e.g., GAO, 2012).

---

identifying individuals who are medically capable of completing training and initial contracted term of service and performing job duties without aggravating existing physical defects or medical conditions. This DoDI also specifies that members are expected to be medically adaptable to the military environment without geographical area limitations (i.e., be ready to deploy worldwide).

[5] Although we couch this discussion within a pilot program framework, many of these measures can be used and analyzed within each system to identify areas of improvement.

Effectiveness

Although we list two effectiveness outcomes in the logic model (Figure 5.1), the two outcomes combined address system accuracy and reliability: whether the system consistently and correctly identifies those who are medically fit to serve and those who are not. A key output tied to effectiveness outcomes would therefore involve the qualification decisions made about the applicants in the system.

To examine accuracy of medical qualification decisions, we suggest a measure used by USMEPCOM, which analyzes the reasons why enlisted personnel medically separate during their initial training period. Specifically, USMEPCOM analyzes EPTS attrition data to understand how many enlisted personnel had medical conditions that were not caught during the medical screening process at MEPS. A similar measure could be used for officer applicants, although the time frame for data collection would need to be longer than for enlisted applicants because of the longer amount of time that officers spend at their accession sources.[6]

A measure (and analysis) that would get at reliability of decisionmaking would involve an audit of the medical information used to make the qualification decisions by medical experts who were not involved in those decisions but are familiar with the processes (e.g., previous service medical waiver authorities or retired CMOs). An audit can examine how consistent those making the qualification decisions are and whether certain information was overlooked/missed. This would be a quality-control type of analysis that would look to identify potential ways to improve system reliability.[7]

---

[6] A consideration for officers is the base rate of EPTS attrition. If very few officers separate for medical reasons while at their accession education programs, EPTS attrition analysis might not be useful. We would recommend first getting a sense of the base rate of EPTS attrition for officer accessions before implementing the pilot program. Moreover, EPTS attrition analysis can help identify one type of inaccurate decision: *false positives* (i.e., individuals who were deemed medically qualified to serve but were not). The analysis cannot identify *false negatives* (i.e., individuals who were deemed medically unqualified to serve but were medically qualified).

[7] Although focused on reliability of decisionmaking, an audit analysis could help identify conditions under which false positives and false negatives (i.e., inaccurate qualification decisions) may occur.

Efficiency

Efficiency outcomes focus on timeliness and financial costs. Timeliness metrics include the amount of time needed to process applicants through the medical screening process and the average time it takes for applicants to travel to exam locations. Processing time should begin when applicants first encounter the system (i.e., for DoDMERB, when they get a letter from DoDMERB to schedule exams in the Concorde system; for USMEPCOM, when their recruiters contact MEPS to schedule their medical exams). The processing time ends at the point when a medical decision is made and the applicant is notified.[8] Key decision and contact points should be captured in the processing time analysis, to include specialty consultations and waiver reviews.

A tool such as the one we describe later in this chapter can be used to estimate driving times from applicants' home locations to medical examination locations. For applicants who fly to their examinations, records of their air travel would be used to compute average travel times.

Financial costs can be measured in terms of medical screening costs per applicant. As we indicated in Chapter 3, USMEPCOM has conducted a cost comparison between DoDMERB and USMEPCOM as part of past reform efforts. However, because of differences between the recruiting and medical screening requirements for enlisted and officer applicants, direct comparisons of costs for medical exams are not straightforward. In the case of an RCT for a hybrid model, costs can be compared separately by applicant population, as both populations would be represented in the two systems. We would expect that financial cost estimates per medical exam would account not only for the medical activities but also for processing costs and could be expanded to include other costs, such as travel costs (as noted in the previous paragraph).

---

[8]   In the case of the academies, it is possible that an applicant will challenge a medical disqualification. In such cases, where the service is to reevaluate the medical package for that applicant, the processing "clock" would start again and complete at the point where a final medical qualification decision has been made and the applicant notified.

Another metric of efficiency that combines time and cost considerations would be to calculate the number and complexity of activities involved in each system. For example, the MEPS medical section pre-screens applicants based on paper forms that recruiters submit on their behalf. This labor-intensive step does not occur in the DoDMERB system. However, DoDMERB is faced with IT system challenges on the back end of the medical review process (as briefly outlined in Chapter 3). Each step can be examined in terms of processing times for staff and the labor costs associated with them. Again, because the RCT would randomly assign participants to the two systems, comparisons can be made for enlisted applicants across the two systems and for officer applicants across the two systems.

Experience

Experience outcomes reflect a system that provides applicants with an experience of care and sufficient transparency (positive interpersonal treatment by medical screening personnel, transparency in what is required as part of the screening process, and so on), as well as reduces the burden on other key stakeholders (e.g., recruiters) to the extent possible. Several measures can get at facets of experience (e.g., perceived interpersonal treatment by medical screening staff); these usually involve surveys, interviews, or focus groups with stakeholders and applicants.

Surveys can be cost-effective in that they can reach larger numbers of individuals. However, response rates can be suboptimal. Interviews and focus groups provide more detailed information about useful context for system improvements, but they are more labor intensive. Notionally, a well-designed survey may be the primary method for gathering feedback from applicants and recruiters, and perhaps samples of MEPS medical staff and Concorde providers. However, for stakeholders from the accession sources, service waiver authorities, USMPECOM HQ, and DoDMERB HQ personnel, interviews and/ or focus groups may be a better data collection method because these stakeholders have ongoing contact with the two systems and could provide useful context.

Step 2: Calculate Sample Sizes

The implementation of a pilot program will inevitably require resources and put additional burden on applicants as well as USMEPCOM and DoDMERB personnel. One way to minimize the potential burden is to compute the number of applicants needed to detect the impact of the medical screening options with very high probability. There are some general guidelines about sample sizes required for studies. Fewer applicants are needed if the measure will likely detect a large difference between the groups being compared in the pilot program. Also, more complex analyses and more complex pilot program designs typically mean more participants are needed to detect differences between groups.

The sample sizes required for pilot programs depend on four factors:

1. The characteristics of the measures used to represent the outputs and the outcomes of the pilot program
2. The desired levels of impact that the decisionmakers would like to detect
3. The technical characteristics of the experimental design that is implemented
4. The parameters of statistical analyses that will be applied to the experimental data.

To illustrate how these factors affect the sample size, we use the following example:

1. A binary measure of pass (medically qualified) and fail (medically disqualified)
2. Two potential levels of impact (using DoDMERB as baseline comparison group), such that 25 percent pass and 50 percent pass
3. A simple experimental design whereby applicants are randomly assigned to DoDMERB or to MEPS within a specific geographic region
4. Magnitude of the different passing rates between the two groups (i.e., applicants assigned to MEPS versus those assigned to DoDMERB in the pilot program).

Figure 5.2
Sample Size of Pilot Program Applicants and Magnitude of Impact on Outcome

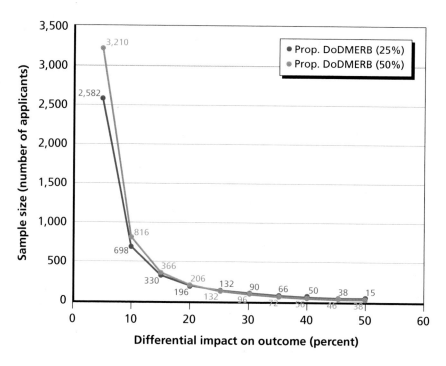

Figure 5.2 illustrates the relationship between required sample size and magnitude of the impact on a pass/fail measure.[9] We show two lines—one that assumes applicants who are being screened through the DoDMERB system pass the medical screening at 25 percent (blue) and one that shows applicants being screened through the DoDMERB system passing at 50 percent (orange). The x-axis shows the differential impact/effect on the outcome of passing the medical screening between DoDMERB and MEPS. For example, the 10 percent on the x-axis means that the applicants who are screened by MEPS pass the

---

[9] We use STATA 15 to compute the sample sizes for a two-sided hypothesis for two proportions based on two independent samples. We accept STATA default values for alpha (0.05), power (0.80), and delta (0.05) associated with the computation. For details, please review the STATA manual.

screen at a level that is 10 percentage points higher than that of applicants screened by DoDMERB. In other words, in this hypothetical example, applicants who are screened by MEPS pass the screen at 35 percent (blue) and 60 percent (orange), versus 25 percent (blue) and 50 percent (orange) for DoDMERB.

As Figure 5.2 shows, fewer applicants are needed to detect a large impact (here, measured by percentage differences between applicants who are screened by MEPS or DoDMERB). To detect a difference of 5 percent between MEPS and DoDMERB pass rates, the pilot program would need over 2,000 applicants, whereas detecting a large difference requires fewer participants (e.g., around 100 participants for a difference of 30 percent). Second, the needed number of applicants varies based on the passing rate for the baseline group, in this case, DoDMERB. For example, if the passing rate for DoDMERB is 25 percent and decisionmakers want to detect a small (5 percent) difference between DoDMERB and MEPS passing rates, 2,582 people are needed in the pilot study. However, if the passing rate for DoDMERB is 50 percent, fewer participants (3,210 total) would be needed to detect a 5-percent difference between DoDMERB and MEPS passing rates. Hence, if we assume a modest (10-percent) difference between passing rates and that DoDMERB's baseline passing rate is 50 percent, we would require at least 816 participants for the pilot program.

As we describe in step 1, the pilot program will have a variety of measurements that will go beyond a simple measure of pass (medically qualified) and fail (medically disqualified). Some of the measurements will produce quantitative variables (e.g., dollar values for medical screening costs). To account for the contributions of different measures on outcomes of interest, the data analysis of the pilot program will include multivariate statistical models. Given this complexity (i.e., multiple measures and statistical modeling), we determine the sample size for the pilot program under different conditions.[10] Among the conditions we examined, the most demanding in terms of sample

---

[10] We assume that there will be four experimental sites. At each site, randomization treatment is completed at the individual level (e.g., randomized to MEPS versus DoDMERB), and the sample is evenly distributed across the four regions. The calculations below indicate the minimum detectible effect size (MDES) for a given sample size. All calculations assume

size is detecting a difference for a binary outcome (yes/no) when the baseline proportion is at one-half (50 percent). We illustrated this in Figure 5.2, which shows that DoD needs approximately 800 applicants to detect a difference of 10 percent for a binary measure. Hence, we recommend that the pilot program should have at least 1,600 applicants (i.e., 800 enlisted applicants and 800 officer applicants).[11] With

---

a false discovery rate of α = 0.05 and power of 0.80 (i.e., an 80-percent chance of detecting the MDES when present; with greater power of detection for larger effects).

Scenario 1: A continuous outcome measure is observed. Without loss of generalization, this outcome is assumed to follow a Standard Normal distribution (mean = 0, standard deviation = 1). Effect size is expressed in number of standard deviations (SD).

Four additional features of the available data impact the MDES calculation:

1. The proportion of variance in the outcome explained by all person-level covariates other than the treatment assignment (i.e., the R^2 of the covariates): without prior knowledge of a covariate (or set of covariates) highly predictive of the set of outcomes that may be considered, we set this conservatively and examine a range between 0.00 and 0.20.
2. The dependency of the observed outcomes within the same region (the intercluster correlation; ICC), due to region-specific influences: we assume such dependencies are small for this exercise and set the ICC to zero. Because the randomization is occurring within regions, the presence of ICC will benefit the statistical power slightly.
3. The heterogeneity of the treatment effect across regions: we assume a constant treatment effect across regions.
4. We consider a fixed-effects model (to accommodate regional influences).

The table below demonstrate the sample size needed (**total**, across all regions and treatment assignments) for generically small- or medium-effect sizes of 0.25 SD and 0.50 SD, respectively.

MDES	R^2		
	0	0.1	0.2
0.25	504	456	404
0.5	128	116	104

Scenario 2: A binary outcome, as in the illustrated example in Figure 5.2, is observed. Because the measures are currently unknown, we plan for multiple binary outcome measures. Therefore, we conservatively assume a baseline proportion of one-half (50 percent), as we have shown in the illustrated example; a baseline proportion much closer to one or zero will require a smaller sample for the same statistical power.

[11] Other conditions (for both continuous/quantitative measures and binary/qualitative measures) require fewer applicants. For example, to detect the same level of difference for the baseline proportion of 25 percent, 698 applicants are needed (but multiplied by two for enlisted and officer).

this number of applicants, the pilot program will have enough statistical power to detect a difference that is less than 0.25 standard deviations (SD) for a continuous/quantitative measure and a difference of 10 percent for a binary measure. These applicants can be divided evenly across the experimental sites.

Step 3: Strategically Select Experimental Sites and Randomly Assign Participants

The final step of the pilot program design is the selection of experimental sites and assignment of the participants. These two activities ensure that the pilot program will yield valid and generalizable findings that decisionmakers can rely on to make policy changes.

Experimental Sites

The organizational and geographic differences among medical screening locations provided by the USMPECOM and DoDMERB systems presents a challenge for selecting experimental sites. For example, while contractors in the DoDMERB system are widely distributed across the country, MEPS are closer to more populated areas. Therefore, applicants who live in rural or less populated areas travel farther distances to receive their medical screening at a MEPS. Another example of a challenge is within the USMEPCOM system itself: Large MEPS may be able to absorb an increase in applicants, but an increase in applicants may create an administrative burden for relatively small MEPS.

Given these kinds of differences, our approach to site selection involved a balance of two competing goals: (1) Minimize systematic biases that can invalidate the results due to intrinsic differences across the sites, and (2) maximize the generalizability of the results by selecting sites that represent variability among the sites. On the one hand, if selected sites are very different in their characteristics (e.g., size, efficiency), it would be difficult to compare the results across the sites. On the other hand, if the selected sites do not represent the variety of available sites, the results from the pilot program will not be generalizable. To balance these competing goals, we include geographical and organizational characteristics as criteria in the site selection process. We also used a systematic analytical approach to select sites. Specifically, we conducted a cluster analysis to identify four relatively homogeneous groups of MEPS stations.[12] We include the following factors associated with each MEPS in the cluster analysis:[13]

1. Number of officer applicants in the zip code
2. Number of enlisted applicants in the zip code
3. Number of medical check-ins
4. Median wait time
5. Average driving time[14]
6. Longitude and latitude.

These factors represent the potential demand for the service, relative efficiency, accessibility, and geography. The clusters are shown in Figure 5.3.

---

[12] Cluster analysis identifies groups of items (in this case, MEPS) that are relatively similar on a set of characteristics. See Appendix D for the theory behind cluster analysis. Our cluster analysis focuses on MEPS because they are relatively stable in terms of locations and features (e.g., size). Also, because there are fewer MEPS than DoDMERB contract locations, MEPS geographically restrict where a pilot program can be conducted.

[13] We used our GIS tool to conduct the cluster analysis and to create factors used in the analysis. The tool incorporates aggregate-level administrative data provided by USMEPCOM and DoDMERB to the RAND team. Data provided by USMEPCOM included FY 2016 information about each MEPS, such as total number of enlisted applicants processed (including those who ultimately do not access), total number of examinations, number of medical disqualifications, top 20 medical categories, total number of medical waivers, MEPS medical station time, number of medical check-ins, and time applicants spent in the medical section (in hours and seconds). DoDMERB provided data from July 2015 through December 2016 on officer applicant zip codes, officer applicant accession source (e.g., Air Force Academy), and Concorde contract provider location zip codes. We conducted sensitivity analyses to determine the stability of the clusters by varying the factors we include in the analysis. Since we found that the definition and membership of these clusters are quite stable, we decided to keep the number of factors relatively few. The primary reason is available factors are highly correlated with the factors we included in the analysis.

[14] We used Google's drive-distance data and zip code–level data to compute average driving times for officer applicants to drive to MEPS. We focused on officer drive times because officer applicants would be expected to have more negative effects for driving time if assigned to the experimental condition (i.e., assigned to a MEPS) than would enlisted applicants assigned to the experimental condition (i.e., assigned to contract locations).

Figure 5.3
Four Homogeneous Clusters of Military Entrance Processing Stations

Table 5.4 shows the average values of MEPS characteristics for each cluster. The clusters tend to group based on two dimensions: capacity and efficiency. For example, the first cluster handles relatively fewer medical check-ins with longer wait time. Cluster 2 on the other hand handles relatively more medication check-ins and with a greater efficiency than Cluster 1. Cluster 3 handles the greatest number of

Table 5.4
Characteristics of Four Clusters of Military Entrance Processing Stations

Cluster	Total Officer	Total Enlisted	# of Medical Check-ins	Median Wait Time (Minutes)	Average Driving Time (Minutes)	Region
1	1,746.33	2,812.42	4,451.92	155.85	95.65	Central
2	2,229.58	3,321.47	6,278.47	85.96	70.1	Mostly North
3	5,832.62	9,445.31	17,215.38	98.12	76.94	Mostly Southwest
4	4,038.11	6,417.39	11,188.11	123.49	73.2	East

medical check-ins but still manages to provide efficient wait time. Finally, Cluster 4 handles the second most check-ins but also has the second longest wait time. The officer applicants living near the MEPS in Cluster 1 are expected to drive the longest time compared to their counterparts living near other MEPS.

We recommend four MEPS as the geographical centers of the experimental sites for the pilot program. They are (1) Louisville, Kentucky; (2) Springfield, Massachusetts; (3) San Diego, California; and (4) Cleveland, Ohio. We selected these sites as representative of their respective clusters. Technically, we computed "distances" between individual MEPS and the centroid of the cluster with which they are associated.[15] The MEPS with the smallest distance from each of the cluster centroids was then taken as a representative of the associated cluster. Table 5.5 provides characteristics of the four MEPS.

Participants

After strategically choosing experimental sites based on clusters and density of applicants, applicants would be randomly assigned to a medical screening option at each experimental site.[16] GAO (2009, p. 4) describes the rationale for this approach:

Table 5.5
Characteristics of MEPS Recommended for Pilot Program

City	Total Officer	Total Enlisted	# of Medical Check-ins	Median Wait Time (Minutes)	Average Driving Time (Minutes)
Louisville	2,191	3,715	6,142	247	66
Springfield	3,484	5,063	11,959	35	73
San Diego	5,362	8,492	18,921	56	96
Cleveland	3,719	5,459	10,550	140	42

---

[15] We applied an approach described in Baralis, Cerquitelli, and D'Elia (2007).

[16] There are different methods for random assignment. Simple random assignment involves assigning participants to groups based on a random-number scheme and without consideration of other factors (e.g., characteristics of the participant population). Other random assignment methods are more complex and may account for participant/study characteris-

Concern about the quality of social program evaluation has led to calls for greater use of randomized experiments—a method used more widely in evaluations of medical than social science interventions. Randomized controlled trials (or randomized experiments) compare the outcomes for groups that were randomly assigned either to the treatment or to a nonparticipating control group before the intervention, in an effort to control for any systematic difference between the groups that could account for a difference in their outcomes. A difference in these groups' outcomes is believed to represent the program's input.

In the context of a pilot program, as depicted in Figure 5.4, the "treatment" is for an applicant to be medically screened in the system in which he or she would not normally be screened (e.g., DoDMERB for enlisted applicants), while the nonparticipating control group consists of applicants who undergo the current screening process (e.g., MEPS for enlisted applicants). The same metrics would be measured for both "treated" and "control" groups. Any observed differences in

Figure 5.4
Random Assignment of Applicants to MEPS or DoDMERB for Medical Screening

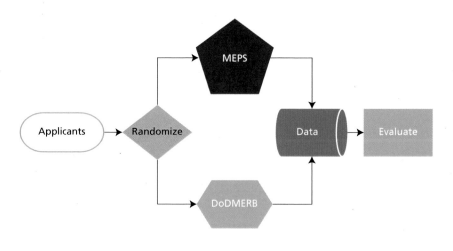

tics and/or sequencing (i.e., when participants enter the program). For a general overview of random assignment methods in experiments, see Suresh (2011).

outcomes can provide valid evidence for policymakers to reform the medical screening process since potential confounding factors—characteristics of MEPS, geographical regions, and unobserved characteristics—are controlled by the design of the pilot program.

Cost Considerations for a Pilot Program

Each of the three stages for designing a pilot program will require time and financial resources to execute. We do not estimate costs because they could vary greatly, depending on the scope of the program. However, in Table 5.6, we do outline key factors that will affect pilot costs by design phase, as well as costs for two phases of pilot program execution—namely, data collection and analysis.

Table 5.6
Factors Affecting Costs by Stage of Pilot Program

Stage	Factors Affecting Pilot Study Costs
1. Determine and develop measures for desired outcomes and outputs	This may be one of the costliest stages of the pilot program. Two key factors can affect costs: 1. **Stakeholder involvement in the process.** The extent to which meetings or workshops would be needed to engage relevant stakeholders (USMEPCOM, DoDMERB, officer accession sources, recruiting commands/services) in ensuring that they do not object to the pilot program goals and design features and organizing and running those meetings could incur significant costs. 2. **Measurement development.** While a pilot program can use existing data (e.g., number of physical exams completed), measures will need to be developed for other data not already available. In particular, surveys, interviews, or focus groups with the applicants in the pilot program would assess applicant perceptions about the medical screening process. The cost of developing the survey or interview/focus group protocol would depend on their complexity (e.g., how many questions are asked) as well as the type and level of labor (e.g., civilian vs. contractor) involved.
2. Calculate sample size	The cost associated with computing the sample size is nominal. The cost of this step comes from the actual sample size used in the study. Sample size will affect the pilot program's administrative costs (e.g., cost of fielding a questionnaire) and potentially the costs of administering the medical exams if one system's exams cost more than the other's exams.

Table 5.6—Continued

Stage	Factors Affecting Pilot Study Costs
3. Site selection and participant assignment	Costs associated with final site selection may be nominal if key stakeholders do not have any issues with the sites identified for inclusion. The main cost will be in the logistics involving assignment of applicants to locations. Other costs will be administrative setup at the locations, once selected.
4. Collect data	Data collection will be one of the costlier stages along with Stage 1 and possibly Stage 3 (in terms of logistics of assigning participants to experimental conditions at each location). For existing data (e.g., number of physical exams performed), data collection costs will be limited to data cleaning and data retrieval from the databases where they reside.[a] For new data, collection costs will depend on how the measures are administered for the pilot study. For example, a questionnaire could be administered on a computer, in person, by mail, or by phone. Computer-based questionnaires would incur costs for programming the questionnaire and ensuring information security, whereas in-person or phone administration would incur labor costs for those administering the questionnaires. Mailing questionnaires would incur postal costs and processing costs to send out and receive the questionnaires.
5. Analyze the data	As with measure development in Stage 1, analysis of the data from the pilot program will incur costs that will depend on type of labor used to perform the analysis and the complexity of the analysis being performed. With multiple measures being employed and different locations for pilot participation, statistical analyses are likely required, which will increase the need for statistical analytical expertise.

NOTE: [a] An exception to this would be data that are available only on paper or scanned documents that are not machine readable. Using these data might require hand entry or text-mining software, which incur labor costs.

A pilot program, particularly one using an RCT design, can be costly. Under the circumstances, DoD may wish to pursue other options. One option is to expand the USMC OCC/PLC program to other accession sources, perhaps at a select number of locations, and assess how well this expanded program meets desired outcomes. Essentially, this would be another type of pilot program but without the random assignment of participants to experimental conditions. Without random assignment, costs associated with the logistics of assigning participants to conditions would not be as much of an issue as with an RCT. Moreover, if this program were treated as optional (e.g., the service academies were given the option to use the program or not), we would expect less time spent on stakeholder coordination than in the case of an RCT.

However, other costs would remain. Measures and metrics would still need to be developed, and data would need to be collected and analyzed. Ironically, data analysis for a non-RCT pilot program could be more complicated (and expensive) than for an RCT pilot program: More factors would need to be statistically controlled in a non-RCT program because participants would not have been randomly assigned to conditions (i.e., cannot rule out selection bias).

Summary

In this chapter, we describe three steps for designing an RCT-based pilot program of a hybrid model, and we provide a discussion of cost considerations for such a program.

The first step is determining and developing measures for the desired system outcomes and outputs. Outcomes generally fall into the three categories of effectiveness, efficiency, and experience. Outputs are the direct and immediate products of the system's inputs and activities. We recommended measures and metrics that align with outcomes and outputs identified in our logic model for an accession medical screening system and could be used in a RCT pilot program of a hybrid system.

The second step of pilot program design is to calculate the number of participants (sample size) needed to meet the program objectives. Sample sizes depend on measure characteristics, desired level of impact to detect with the analysis of measures, program design features, and the type of statistical analyses to be conducted with the data from the pilot program. In general, more complicated measures, designs, and analyses require larger sample sizes. We estimated that the RCT pilot program would require a minimum of 800 enlisted and 800 officer applicants.

The last step of pilot program design involves strategically selecting the locations (sites) for conducting the program and then randomly assigning participants to the experimental groups. Two general criteria should guide the selection of experimental sites: (1) geographical characteristics and (2) organizational characteristics. Using these criteria and conducting an analysis with our GIS tool's cluster analysis capability, we suggest a pilot program that is geographically centered on these four MEPS: Louisville, Kentucky; Springfield, Massachusetts; San Diego, California; and Cleveland, Ohio.

The financial costs associated with this kind of pilot program will vary considerably, depending on stakeholder engagement, developing measures (e.g., surveys), logistics of assigning participants to experimental conditions, data collection (and who will do the collecting), and statistical analyses. DoD may choose to forgo an RCT pilot program and instead expand the USMC OCC/PLC program to other accession sources. This kind of expanded program could reduce costs associated with logistics of participant assignment and stakeholder engagement. However, any evaluative program incurs costs for developing measures and for collecting and analyzing the data associated with those measures.

CHAPTER SIX

Conclusions

In this chapter, we summarize key findings from the study and offer two related recommendations for DoD to consider for updating the business models of the two main systems for accession medical screening processes.

Summary of Key Findings

Stakeholders identified challenges with the current systems, but each system has relative advantages and disadvantages. "Customers" of the USMEPCOM and DoDMERB systems (i.e., enlisted recruiters and AMEDD recruiting representatives for MEPS, and service academy admissions and ROTC admissions for DoDMERB) identified challenges they experience with the respective systems. These include a lack of consistency across MEPS sites and the time required to visit a MEPS for screening (USMEPCOM "customer" concern), and the uncertain quality of reports from civilian providers (DoDMERB "customer" concern). Additionally, when asked about potentially combining the two systems, USMEPCOM and DoDMERB stakeholders expressed concerns about sending their applicants to the other organization's system. These concerns ranged from insufficient quality of examinations provided by Concorde medical providers (USMEPCOM concern) to the inconvenience of officer applicants going to MEPS (DoDMERB concern).

Based on our review of the two systems and these findings from USMEPCOM and DoDMERB stakeholders, we summarize the pri-

Table 6.1
Relative Advantages and Disadvantages of the DoDMERB and USMEPCOM Systems

	DoDMERB	USMEPCOM
Advantages	• Greater number of locations decreases travel time and cost requirements • Online scheduling convenience • Less potential for wait time at exams • Civilian medical exam environment is familiar to applicants	• Exams conducted by medical providers trained in and regularly exposed to accession medicine • Serves as a one-stop shop for numerous pre-accession functions for enlisted applicants • System designed to process large number of applicants
Disadvantages	• Private physicians have less exposure to accession medicine than at MEPS • Serves only medical mission; applicants must go elsewhere for other pre-accession requirements • System currently designed for limited number of applicants	• Fewer locations result in increased travel time and cost • Lack of online scheduling convenience • Greater potential for wait time at exam • Military medical exam environment is unfamiliar to some applicants and may not be well received

mary advantages and disadvantages of each system relative to one another in Table 6.1.

DoD continues to work toward reforming the accessions medical screening systems. To this day, DoD has working groups (e.g., AMWG) and efforts to reform aspects of accessions medical screening processes. One of the largest reforms being attempted is MHS GENESIS, an electronic health record system for MHS. Other reforms involve standardizing forms used in medical screening processes, identifying data needs for the systems, and even pilot studies led by USMEPCOM to address concerns about nondisclosure of relevant medical information.

DoDMERB and USMEPCOM are also invested in improvements to the data management systems used in medical screening processes. However, those efforts are ongoing, and prior attempts at such reforms have not succeeded.

Ongoing efforts at reform presume that DoDMERB and USMEPCOM will continue employing their business models for accession medical screening systems.

Prior efforts to reform the two systems' business models have not been fully implemented or had unclear outcomes. Although ongoing efforts at reform are not focused on changing DoDMERB's and USMEPCOM's business models for accession medical screening systems, DoD has attempted to pilot such efforts in the past. Information on past pilot programs (e.g., West Virginia and Tennessee pilot studies) is limited, making it difficult to discern why these programs were not fully implemented. Information from DoDMERB and USMEPCOM experts who were involved or knew about these past pilot studies suggest that they did not work because of information-sharing issues and changes in leadership. In at least one case—a program implemented by the Army National Guard to use "hometown" medical providers to conduct the accession medical screening—USMEPCOM experts cite issues with the quality of the information from those providers as a reason the program was stopped.

There is one program involving USMC's OCC/PLC applicants use of either DoDMERB or USMEPCOM systems for medical screening that continues to this date. However, we were unable to get enough data from USMC, DoDMERB, and USMEPCOM to evaluate the program's outcomes. Moreover, the program does not currently lend itself to answering questions about how well it would generalize to other accession sources. The program would need to be expanded to other accession sources to determine how well it would work.

All three COAs for reforming the business models of the two systems could have major impacts on DoDMERB and/or USMEPCOM. The two business models are distinct: DoDMERB outsources medical screening at nongovernmental facilities, while USMEPCOM uses government personnel (with some outsourcing) to conduct medical screenings on-site at MEPS (which are governmental facilities). We developed three COAs to reflect this continuum of outsourcing: (1) High Outsource, (2) Low Outsource, and (3) Mix of Both (i.e., a Hybrid model). We also identified variants of COAs. Using the three criteria of organization, capacity, and information sharing, we assessed the potential level of impact of each COA on DoDMERB and USMEPCOM.

Each COA could have major impacts on the two systems but in different ways. A high outsource COA (COA 1) that puts all medical screening under DoDMERB would significantly impact USMEPCOM (as its medical screening function would drop significantly) and DoDMERB (which would need to significantly increase capacity for an influx of enlisted applicants). A low outsource COA (COA 2) that puts all medical screening under USMEPCOM would not have a major impact on USMEPCOM given the size of its current mission, but it would effectively remove DoDMERB from the accession medical mission. The third COA for a hybrid model in which enlisted and officer applicants can go to DoDMERB or USMEPCOM will have major impacts on capacity to the extent that applicants (and their recruiters) have the freedom to choose locations. However, regardless of the level of choice given to applicants in COA 3, we would expect major impacts on DoDMERB's and USMEPCOM's information-sharing requirements because both organizations would need to be able to communicate with all of the various stakeholders involved in both systems.

Although COA 3 could have major impacts, it may be the least risky of the three COAs for DoD to adopt. Unlike COAs 1 and 2, COA 3 is not designed to significantly disrupt the organizational structures and staffing of MEPS or DoDMERB (although we note that focusing resources on one organization may be more efficient). COA 3 is also the only COA that would allow population cross-flows (i.e., some enlisted applicants going through DoDMERB system while some officer applicants who would usually go through DoDMERB now going through MEPS). Finally, COA 3 has a template in the USMC OCC/PLC program that DoD could consider expanding to other accession sources.

Pilot programs can help DoD assess COA 3 impacts. Because of the complexities involved in adopting a COA, we describe a three-step approach to design pilot programs to test COA 3 features of interest to policy makers. The three steps for pilot program design are: (1) determine and develop measures for desired outputs and outcomes,

(2) calculate sample sizes, and (3) strategically select experimental sites and randomly assign participants. For the first step, we identified three categories of outcomes (effectiveness, efficiency, and experience) and recommended specific outcomes and outputs (e.g., medical readiness to serve as an outcome and medical qualification decisions as an output), as well as measures and metrics (e.g., analyzing EPTS attrition data). For the second step, we provided an example of a simple, binary (pass/fail) measure to demonstrate the complexities of sample size calculations. We then calculated a sample size of 1,600 participants (800 enlisted and 800 officers) for the pilot program. For the third and final design step, we took into account the features of MEPS locations (e.g., size) and characteristics of the applicant population and conducted a cluster analysis to identify groups (clusters) of MEPS sites. We identified four clusters of MEPS and selected four MEPS (Louisville, Kentucky; Springfield, Massachusetts; San Diego, California; and Cleveland, Ohio) to represent those clusters. Once sites are selected, participants in the pilot program would be randomly assigned to "control" and "treatment" (or "intervention") groups.

Recommendations

Based on our key findings, we offer two related recommendations: (1) DoD should adopt a hybrid model (COA 3) but conduct pilot programs to test it, and (2) DoD should ensure conditions are favorable for pilot program success.

Test and Adopt a Hybrid Model

We recommend that DoD adopt COA 3 for a hybrid of USMEPCOM and DoDMERB systems for accessions medical screening processes. We base this recommendation on the arguments we lay out in Chapter 4 and summarized earlier in this chapter: COA 3 is less risky than COAs 1 and 2 because it does not require either system to significantly modify organizational structure and staff; it has a template in the USMC OCC/PLC program; and it allows simultaneous testing of the cross-flows of enlisted and officer applicants across the two systems.

Because each of the two current systems has advantages and disadvantages, the ultimate goal for COA 3 is to optimize advantages across the two systems. To do that, we propose DoD first pilot test a hybrid model at the four geographic locations identified in Chapter 5 (Louisville, Kentucky; Springfield, Massachusetts; San Diego, California; and Cleveland, Ohio) and use random assignment of participants to rule out selection bias (i.e., conduct an RCT). However, an RCT can fail if conditions are not favorable for conducting such a pilot program. Therefore, our next recommendation is that DoD ensure conditions are favorable for pilot program success.

Ensure Conditions Are Favorable for Pilot Program Success

As discussed in prior chapters, it is challenging to evaluate the impact of changes in policies and practices without implementing the principles of program evaluation. A successful pilot program will allow policymakers to determine what features of accession medical screening systems have the greatest impact on outputs and outcomes consistent with their objectives for these systems.

In the previous chapter, we provided detailed aspects of an RCT-based pilot program that DoD can implement. However, before implementing a pilot program, we caution DoD to heed the lessons of past pilot reform efforts as well as ongoing programs. We briefly outline key lessons from past reform efforts:

- Clearly articulate objectives for the pilot program to key stakeholders to ensure their buy-in.
- Ensure continuity so that as leaders involved with the pilot program leave their positions, successors can see the pilot program through.
- Understand impact of a pilot program on ongoing efforts at reform, particularly involving systems for information sharing and management (e.g., electronic health records system). Ideally, new information-sharing systems would be in place by the time a pilot program is launched, but if that is not the case, DoD will need to understand the potential effects on pilot program results. DoD would also need to establish alternative information-sharing arrangements in the pilot program.

In addition to these lessons, DoD should validate our assumptions and, if necessary, recompute our estimates. At a minimum, USMEPCOM and DoDMERB should confirm if the four sites we recommend for the pilot program are viable and would not disrupt other activities (e.g., other pilot programs).

Even if DoD were to heed lessons of the past to create conditions favorable to pilot program success, the costs of developing and implementing an RCT-based pilot program may be high enough that DoD chooses an alternative path. For example, DoD might instead conduct a non-RCT pilot program that expands the USMC OCC/PLC program to other accession sources, which could reduce costs associated with randomly assigning participants to experimental sites and the stakeholder engagement that entails. Alternatively, DoD might forgo any kind of pilot program and instead focus on its ongoing efforts to improve accession medical screening processes within the existing business models used by USMEPCOM and DoDMERB. Although we do not provide precise cost estimates for these options, all options have associated costs. Expanding the USMC OCC/PLC program would still require measure development, data collection, and data analysis. Some of the ongoing reform efforts, such as the move toward an electronic health record system (MSH GENESIS), could have significant up-front costs, as would any new data management system.

Before eschewing the idea of an RCT-based pilot program, DoD should determine if an alternative pilot program based on the USMC OCC/PLC program or just continuing with ongoing reform efforts will sufficiently address key objectives for an updated and modernized accession medical screening system. A well-executed pilot program should give policymakers considerable insight into whether significant changes to where and how officer and enlisted applicants receive their accession medical screening provides a more effective, more efficient, and viable option for screening that can be introduced nationwide to all branches of the services.

Focus Group and Interview Methodology

Focus Groups

To understand recruiters' perspectives and experiences with the USMEPCOM system, the RAND project team conducted ten focus groups with recruiters across the military services, including active-duty and reserve component recruiters primarily in the broader Los Angeles and Washington, D.C., metropolitan areas. These recruiters represented a mix of urban, rural, and suburban areas to ensure input captured the unique challenges of each of these recruiting environments. Table A.1 outlines the range of recruiting environments across the service components included in the focus group sample.

RAND asked participating recruiting offices for approximately five to eight volunteers for each focus group, although some focus groups included slightly fewer participants when based in smaller recruiting offices. Focus group facilitators administered informed consent at the start of each focus group, emphasizing the voluntary nature of participation and assuring participant confidentiality. We asked focus group participants about their experiences using the USMEPCOM system and visiting MEPS locations, including any related challenges they experienced as recruiters. Once all focus groups were completed, RAND researchers analyzed focus group notes to identify key themes and trends regarding recruiters' experiences with MEPS.

Table A.1
Focus Group Components and Recruiting Environments

Component	Urban	Suburban	Rural
Army	X	X	
Marine Corps		X	X
Navy	X	X	
Air Force	X	X	X
Air Force Reserve	X	X	X
Army National Guard	X	X	X
Air National Guard	X	X	X

NOTE: Air Force Reserve is a separate recruiting command for the Air Force. Reserve recruiting is included with active-duty recruiting for the other military services. National Guard recruiting is separate for both the Army and Air Force.

Interviews

RAND also held discussions with approximately 35 experts, some in groups, from summer 2016 through spring 2017. We do not provide a precise number of participants because some participants invited colleagues who listened but did not contribute to the discussion or provided limited input. Interviews were in person or over the phone, most lasting an hour or less.

Participants represented a variety of organizations or entities in DoD, including AMWG, DoD Health Affairs, DoDMERB, OUSD/P&R/MPP (AP), officer accession sources (service academies, service ROTCs), service waiver authorities, AMEDD, USAREC, and USMEPCOM. We initially worked with our project sponsor to identify key stakeholders to contact regarding interview participation. Beyond that, we relied on the snowball sampling method, in which interviewees suggested additional individuals or organizations that would be important for us to interview and include in the study.

Discussions were semistructured in nature, but the protocols varied by type of stakeholder. With DoDMERB and USMEPCOM, we focused on learning about their current regulations, policies, and practices, as well as what they consider to be limitations to adopting the business model of the other medical screening system.

Discussions with officer accession sources covered how the accession sources process their applicants and where DoDMERB screening occurs in the overall admissions process. We also asked about any challenges they might have experienced with medical screening processes and whether they would consider participating in a pilot program.

Discussions with service waiver authorities focused on their processes and engagement with MEPS medical departments or DoDMERB.

Discussions with AMEDD and USAREC focused on recruiting and medical screening for medical professionals (e.g., physicians) into the U.S. Army because those individuals are medically screened at MEPS, unlike officer applicants to the U.S. Military Academy (West Point) or Army ROTC.

Discussions with DoD Health Affairs focused specifically on the Reserve Health Readiness Program (RHRP), which uses contract medical providers to perform periodic health assessments for reservists. The intent of learning about RHRP was to determine how it compares to the DoDMERB contract model. While the discussions provided useful information about RHRP, we determined that the comparison was not necessary for the purposes of the project given the different purpose, timeline, and population for RHRP compared with accession medical screening, mostly of individuals who are new to the military (non-prior service accessions).

Finally, we discussed ongoing efforts of AMRG and other DoD working groups with OUSD/P&R/MPP (AP) experts who are involved with these groups. We also spoke with other members of the AMWG not in OUSD/P&R/MPP (AP). Once all interviews were complete, we analyzed the detailed interview notes to identify the key themes and qualitative findings that we have reported in earlier chapters.

Design Workshop Methodology

This appendix provides a brief overview of the methodology used for the design workshop described in Chapter 5, including how the team reviewed the outputs from the workshop to inform the sample pilot program design.

Participant Solicitation

To solicit participants, we worked with the sponsor's office to identify relevant stakeholder organizations besides the ones we had identified in earlier project activities (e.g., USMEPCOM). Since many of the key organizations are represented in AMWG, our sponsor's office arranged for us to speak to AMWG at its June 2017 meeting. At the meeting, we explained the purpose of the project and the goal of the workshop. We asked the members to suggest individuals from their organizations to attend the workshop, which we said would be held in August or September. Interested parties emailed project team members directly to indicate interest. The project team coordinated schedules and selected dates for the workshop. September 15, 2017, was chosen as one that would work best for the largest number of potential participants.

Workshop Agenda

The project team developed a presentation and agenda for the workshop. The team used key components of a logic model (described in

Chapter 5) to solicit feedback from participants. The primary purpose of the workshop was for experts on accession medical screening processes and related activities (e.g., recruiting) to identify outcomes, outputs, and inputs for an accession medical screening system. The information they provided was used to modify the logic model for such a system and identify considerations for designing a pilot study to evaluate changes to the two business models used for accession medical screening systems.

The project team provided information about the workshop and the project to the experts. The team facilitated most activities although the project sponsor outlined the strategic objectives of a pilot (which align with the broad questions outlined in Chapter 5) after opening remarks by the team. Table B.1 shows the workshop agenda.

Three key members of the project team facilitated the workshop. Each member has extensive experience facilitating focus groups and workshops. During the workshop activities in which participants inputs were requested (see right column of Table B.1), one team member facilitated the activity while another member typed notes on a slide that was projected on a screen for all participants to see. These activities included a demonstration of a RAND GIS tool to solicit feedback from the workshop participants. (See Chapter 5 and Appendix D for more details about the GIS tool.) Two other junior team members who did not help facilitate the workshop took notes of the discussion on their laptops for later review by the project team.

Post-Workshop Review

The team used an iterative process to identify relevant themes from the workshop. The two junior team members first summarized themes from their extensive notes and sent them to senior team members for review. The senior team members who facilitated the workshop collectively identified the key categories of factors recommended by participants and which of those align to the six logic model components. Factors that did not fit with the logic model components largely fell into the area of implementation considerations (logistics) for a pilot.

Table B.1
Design Workshop Agenda

Time Frame	Activity	Facilitator/Participant
8:00–8:30	`Check-In	
8:30–8:45	Welcome, Opening Remarks, and Introductions	• RAND
8:45–9:00	Strategic Objectives of Pilot	• OSD Accession Policy
9:00–9:30	Past Reform Efforts and Stakeholder Input on Current Processes	• RAND
9:30–10:30	Discussion: Outcomes of Medical Accessions System	• RAND • Discussion with workshop participants
10:30–10:45	Break	
10:45–11:45	Discussion: Conceptual Outline of Pilot	• RAND • Discussion with workshop participants
11:45–12:15	Break for lunch	
12:15–1:00	RAND Analytic Tool Demonstration	• RAND • Discussion with workshop participants
1:00–1:15	Break	
1:15–1:30	Summary and Next Steps	• RAND

NOTE: Workshop time frames are in Eastern Time.

For example, a participant mentioned the need to ensure that the applicants who normally go through DoDMERB are registered properly in the IT system used for the pilot program. Another participant mentioned making sure the commanders of the MEPS where the pilot program takes place are aware of and support the program. While these are important considerations for ensuring the pilot program is implemented, they do not signify major system design changes. However, these kinds of considerations are noted in our recommendation for enabling conditions to ensure pilot program success (Chapter 6).

Logic Model for Accession Medical Screening System

This appendix provides a detailed logic model for an accession medical screening system. We developed the model based on workshop participant feedback regarding outcomes, outputs, and inputs. We supplemented the workshop feedback with our review of the current systems, particularly so we could describe the system activities. We added contextual factors based on broad considerations of the national security, military, and external environment that would affect many DoD systems.

We first describe the logic model and provide some examples of how its components relate to accession medical screening processes. We follow with a table summarizing what workshop participants provided and how we used their feedback in the logic model.

Description of Logic Model Components

The detailed logic model is depicted in Figure 5.1 in Chapter 5, so we do not repeat it here. However, we provide more detail on the components of the logic model below.

Context factors affect the entire system, but mostly through indirect means (via effects on inputs). *Security Strategy and Doctrine* refers to the high-level direction for national defense as outlined in U.S. strategy documents at the national level down to the military service level (e.g., National Security Strategy, NDS, Army Strategic Planning Guidance). Doctrine is derived from strategy and provides guidance for military operations. For example, strategies and doctrine may direct the focus on missions to address cybersecurity threats.

Environment refers to both national security (e.g., terrorism threats) and nonsecurity factors that could affect accessions and in turn medical screening processes. For example, a tight civilian labor market makes it more difficult for the military services to recruit. If the services do not make their recruiting missions, there are fewer individuals who need medical screening.

Resources and Requirements refer to what is needed (requirements) and what is provided (resources) to support DoD and the services in executing their core missions. For example, DoD may use funding from Congress to acquire a new IT system that can support accession medical screening processes.

Force structure refers to how each military service organizes its personnel and equipment to complete core missions. Force structure changes can spur new accessions requirements, including changes to the number of individuals needed for the mission as well as medical requirements that would need to be included in the screening process.

Inputs are resources needed to execute and evaluate an accession medical screening system. We identify four categories of inputs: *Materiel* (i.e., equipment and materials needed for medical screening and qualification processes), *Personnel* (staff required to conduct medical screening, conduct waiver reviews, perform administrative functions, set relevant policy and oversight, and so on), *Facilities* (i.e., where medical screening is conducted and relevant staff work), and *Policy and Regulations* (e.g., USMEPCOM regulations for conducting medical screening, DoD's accession medical standards, each service's recruiting policies).

Activities refer to the actions to design, develop, and implement the system. We outline two categories of activities: *Recruiting and Admissions* and *Medical Screening.* The first category refers to activities conducted by recruiters, academy admissions offices, and other service accession sources to prepare applicants for medical screening at MEPS or through DoDMERB. *Medical Screening* activities are conducted primarily by USMEPCOM and DoDMERB staff (including contractors) to evaluate applicants' medical fitness for service. However, the services' medical waiver review authorities are also involved in the medical screening process when medical waivers are required.

Outputs are the direct and immediate results of inputs and activities. *Throughput* refers to the number and type of applicants processed and medical qualification determinations that are made, as well as time and process elements for conducting the system activities. *Stakeholder Reactions* are the perceptions and experiences of individuals who go through the system (applicants) as well as direct customers of the systems, namely accession sources.

Outcomes are longer-term effects of the system. They are what should drive system design, execution, and evaluation decisions. Outcomes are usually thought of in terms of how well the system meets desired objectives (*Effectiveness*) and how many resources are required to meet those objectives (*Efficiency*). Effectiveness refers to "quality" of medical decisions (i.e., system correctly identifies those who are medically fit to serve and those who are not) and the ultimate goal of having a force that is ready to serve (which includes the component of medical readiness). Efficiency outcomes are those that are aligned with using the least amount of resources to achieve the effectiveness objectives. In our logic model, we also include *Experience* to represent customer satisfaction, or how well key stakeholders (applicants, recruiters, accession sources, and so on) believe the system meets their needs.

Evaluation can involve any of the factors within most components of the logic model, but the flow of evaluations goes from inputs and activities (i.e., what goes into the system) to outputs and outcomes (i.e., what comes out of the system). Because context falls outside a system owner's control, it is not a central part of system evaluation (which is why we do not have an arrow from context to evaluation in the logic model figure).[1]

---

[1] Although contextual factors are outside the system, evaluations of parts of the system may try to control for contextual factors. For example, an analysis of the relationships among personnel factors (inputs) and throughput (outputs) may involve controlling for labor market trends, which are part of context.

Our description of pilot program design in Chapter 5 would be one way to test major changes to factors in the logic model. However, evaluation (especially as the current systems are being maintained) can and does occur without pilot programs. For example, when USMEPCOM wants to know how many med-techs are needed to produce a certain level of throughput, USMEPCOM analysts conduct manpower analyses to evaluate the required number.

Workshop Contributions to Logic Model

As discussed in Chapter 5, we asked workshop participants to describe outcomes, outputs, and inputs for an accession medical screening system. Table 5.2 summarized their recommendations. We repeat that table here (as Table C.1), and add a column to outline how we used the information they provided for developing the logic model depicted in Figure 5.1. As noted in Chapter 5, we do not include all factors described by participants, as some focused on implementation considerations for a pilot effort (e.g., getting support from commanders of MEPS where a pilot program would take place).

Theoretical Background of Cluster Analysis

This appendix outlines the theory behind cluster analysis, which we used to group the MEPS based on their characteristics. As we note in Chapter 5, there are established techniques and tools for finding groups of items that are relatively similar. In the field of machine learning, this area of research is known as *cluster analysis*.

The theoretical underpinning of much of cluster analysis assumes a *generative probabilistic framework*. In other words, and in this application, we would assume that the data describing MEPS were generated by some probabilistic model and then would derive an estimate of that model. For example, let us say we have an n-dimensional feature vector full of descriptive statistics describing a particular MEPS. One model for how each feature vector is generated involves sampling a random variable X drawn from a Gaussian Mixture Model (GMM) (Murphy, 2012). A GMM is a probability distribution that combines k multivariate normal distributions that have specified means, μ_k terms, and given covariance matrices, φ_k. The likelihood of observing a particular feature vector describing a particular MEPS x is the sum of the probabilities of drawing from each of the Gaussians in the mixture, multiplied by the conditional probability of having observed the day record given the specific Gaussian distribution.

Let z be the latent (unobserved) random variable that indicates which Gaussian distribution it was drawn from; this variable has a prior probability distribution $prob\,(z = k) = \pi_k$ with the constraint that $\sum_k \pi_k = 1$ for consistency. The clustering problem is thus recast in the GMM as inferring which of the k clusters or Gaussians the MEPS-specific feature vector *x* was drawn from; in other words, the task of the clustering algorithm is to infer the posterior of the latent variable, the probability that the observed *x* was drawn from cluster *k*, which is determined by Bayes rule and is called the *cluster-responsibility* (Murphy, 2012).

The most famous type of clustering is *k-means clustering*, a form of "hard-clustering" where each data point is assigned to a single cluster. Assignment is based on identifying the largest value among the posterior probabilities mentioned in the preceding paragraph. More generally, however, a clustering algorithm attempts to fit all of the parameters $(\pi_k, \mu_k, \varphi_k)$ using an iterative algorithm such as Expectation-Maximization (EM) to calculate cluster responsibilities. The k-means approach assumes that each of the above clusters has equal and uncorrelated features and that the prior cluster probabilities are uniform, i.e., $\pi_k = 1/k$ (Murphy, 2012). Thus, any inference algorithm (such as EM) needs to only determine cluster centers and assign each MEPS *x* to the closest cluster center. The reduction of the EM algorithm with these assumptions is equivalent to minimizing the objective function

$$\sum_{k}\sum_{x \in C_k} \|x - \mu_k\|_2^2$$

over the cluster centers μ_k, and cluster assignments of each *x* into disjoint sets C_k.

The most commonly used algorithm for k-means clustering alternates between cluster assignment, linking each data point *x* (here, MEP station) with fixed cluster centers by minimizing the Euclidean distance above, and computation of cluster centers, with fixed cluster assignments using the vector-average $\mu_k = (\sum_{x \in C_k} x) / N_k$. The initial assignment of cluster centers can be randomly chosen to be *k* of the *N* data points.

The Euclidean distance calculated using the formula above is typically based on features that are normalized or otherwise scaled attributes of the individual data points, in this case, MEPS. This is particularly true if there is no intuitive reason to think certain attributes are more important than others. Normalization ensures the features are roughly equally important in defining clusters.

Let us say a_{ij} terms represent attribute j of MEPS i, which might be, for example, the number of medical exams performed during a recent year at the MEPS. Then we normalize to yield feature j of facility i: $f_{ij} = (a_{ij} - \mu)/\sigma$, where μ and σ are the average and standard deviation, across the set of all MEPS, of the number of medical exams performed. Normalization ensures the ranges of values are similar for each feature. The distance or dissimilarity between facility i and cluster center k would then be $d_{ik} = \sqrt{\sum_{j} \left(f_{ij} - f_{kj} \right)^2}$.

References

Arendt, Christopher, Acting Director of Accession Policy, "Request for Continued Utilization of the Department of Defense Medical Review Board for Physical Examination Processing for Marine Officer Applicants," memorandum for the Deputy Commandant for Manpower and Reserve Affairs, Washington D.C.: Office of the Assistant Secretary of Defense, Readiness and Force Management, July 16, 2014.

Baralis, Elena, Tania Cerquitelli, and Vincenzo D'Elia, "Modeling a Sensor Network by Means of Clustering," *18th International Conference on Database and Expert Systems Applications (DEXA 2007)*, Washington, D.C., IEEE Computer Society, 2007, pp. 177–181.

Barna, Stephanie, Principal Deputy Assistant Secretary of Defense for Manpower and Reserve Affairs, U.S. Department of Defense, "Inclusion of Accession Organizations into the Defense Healthcare Management System Modernization Program," memorandum to the Director of the Defense Health Agency and the Program Executive Officer for Defense Healthcare Management Systems, Washington, D.C., June 15, 2016.

Campos, Mariano C., Jr., "Commander's Commentary," *Messenger*, Vol. 30, No. 4, 2008, p. 3. As of March 8, 2019:
http://www.mepcom.army.mil/Portals/112/Documents/Messenger/Messenger_Vol_30_No_4.pdf

Concorde, Inc., "Welcome to DoDMETS," 2018. As of August 30, 2018:
https://www.dodmets.com

Department of Defense, *Summary of the 2018 National Defense Strategy of the United States of America: Sharpening the American Military's Competitive Edge*, Washington, D.C.: U.S. Department of Defense, 2018. As of August 30, 2018:
https://dod.defense.gov/Portals/1/Documents/pubs/2018-National-Defense
-Strategy-Summary.pdf

Department of Defense Form 2807-1, "Report of Medical History," U.S. Department of Defense, March 2015. As of August 30, 2018:
http://www.mepcom.army.mil/Portals/112/Documents/PubsForms/Forms/
f-0000-dd-2807-01.pdf

Department of Defense Form 2807-2, "Accessions Medical Prescreen Report," U.S. Department of Defense, March 2015. As of August 30, 2018: http://www.mepcom.army.mil/Portals/112/Documents/PubsForms/Forms/f-0000-dd-2807-02.pdf

Department of Defense Form 2808, "Report of Medical Examination," U.S. Department of Defense, October 2005. As of August 30, 2018: http://www.mepcom.army.mil/Portals/112/Documents/PubsForms/Forms/f-0000-dd-2808.pdf

Department of Defense Instruction 6130.03, *Medical Standards for Appointment, Enlistment, or Induction into the Military Services*, Washington, D.C.: U.S. Department of Defense, May 6, 2018. As of August 30, 2018: http://www.esd.whs.mil/Portals/54/Documents/DD/issuances/dodi/613003p.pdf?ver=2018-05-04-113917-883

Department of Defense Manual 1145.02, *Military Entrance Processing Station (MEPS)*, Washington, D.C.: U.S. Department of Defense, July 23, 2018. As of August 30, 2018: http://www.esd.whs.mil/Portals/54/Documents/DD/issuances/dodm/114502m.pdf?ver=2018-07-23-121425-917

Department of Defense Medical Examination Review Board, FAQs, 2016. As of August 30, 2018: https://dodmerb.tricare.osd.mil/FAQs.aspx

DoD—*See* Department of Defense.

DoDI—*See* Department of Defense Instruction.

DoDMERB—*See* Department of Defense Medical Examination Review Board.

GAO—*See* U. S. Government Accountability Office.

Gerstein, Daniel M., James G. Kallimani, Lauren A. Mayer, Lelia Meshkat, Jan Osburg, Paul K. Davis, Blake Cignarella, and Clifford A. Grammich, *Developing a Risk Assessment Methodology for the National Aeronautics and Space Administration*, Santa Monica, Calif.: RAND Corporation, RR-1537-NASA, 2016. As of April 02, 2019: https://www.rand.org/pubs/research_reports/RR1537.html

Heimbaugh, Nancy, Director of Defense Logistics Agency Acquisition Component Acquisition Executive, letter to the Honorable Daniel Inouye, Chairman of the Committee on Appropriations, U.S. Senate, Fort Belvoir, Va., September 13, 2012.

Johnson, Gaylan, "The Origins of Modern U.S. Military Entrance Standards," *Messenger*, Vol. 30, No. 4, 2008, pp. 4–9. As of March 8, 2019: http://www.mepcom.army.mil/Portals/112/Documents/Messenger/Messenger_Vol_30_No_4.pdf

Manning, Berton, "JCIDS Process: DOTMLPF-P Analysis," *AcqNotes*, 2019. As of April 8, 2019: http://acqnotes.com/acqnote/acquisitions/dotmlpf-analysis

McCaskill, Claire, Chair, Subcommittee on Financial and Contracting Oversight, letter to Admiral Jonathan W. Greenert, Chief of Naval Operations, June 18, 2013. As of March 13, 2019:
https://www.hsgac.senate.gov/imo/media/doc/2013-06-18%20%20Letter%20 from%20CMC%20to%20Navy%20re%20SPAWAR.pdf

McLaughlin, John A., and Gretcehn B. Jordan, "Logic Models: A Tool for Telling Your Program's Performance Story," *Evaluation and Program Planning*, Vol. 22, No. 1, 1999, pp. 65–72.

Medical and Personnel Executive Steering Committee, *Accession Modernization Working Group Charter*, Washington, D.C.: U.S. Department of Defense, April 20, 2015.

Milstead, R. E., Jr., "Request for Continued Utilization of the Department of Defense Medical Review Board for Physical Examination Processing for Marine Officer Applicants," memorandum for Director of Accession Policy, Office of Secretary of Defense, Quantico, Va.: U.S. Marine Corps, June 12, 2014.

Murphy, Kevin, *Machine Learning: A Probabilistic Perspective (Adaptive Computation and Machine Learning)*, Cambridge, Mass.: MIT Press, 2012.

National Research Council, *Assessing Fitness for Military Enlistment: Physical, Medical, and Mental Health Standards*, Washington, D.C.: National Academies Press, 2006. As of August 30, 2018:
https://doi.org/10.17226/11511

Office of the Assistant Secretary of Defense (Health Affairs), *Accession Medical Examination Preliminary Functional Economic Analysis*, Falls Church, Va., BPR 047-012-001, 1994.

Personnel and Readiness Information Management, *Military Accession White Paper*, Washington, D.C.: U.S. Department of Defense, February 26, 2015.

P&R IM—*See* Personnel and Readiness Information Management.

Solution Delivery Division, Defense Health Agency, "Fact Sheet, DMACS, Defense Medical Accessions Computing System," February 2018. As of March 13, 2019:
https://health.mil/Reference-Center/Fact-Sheets/2018/02/01/DMACS-Fact-Sheet

Suresh, K. P., "An Overview of Randomization Techniques: An Unbiased Assessment of Outcome in Clinical Research," *Journal of Human Reproductive Sciences*, Vol. 4, No. 1, 2011, pp. 8–11.

Taylor-Powell, Ellen, and Ellen Henert, *Developing a Logic Model: Teaching and Training Guide*, 2008. As of July 23, 2019:
https://www.alnap.org/system/files/content/resource/files/main/logic-model-guide .pdf

U.S. Government Accountability Office, *Program Evaluation: A Variety of Rigorous Methods Can Help Identify Effective Interventions*, Washington, D.C.: U.S. Government Accountability Office, GAO-10-30, 2009.

U.S. Government Accountability Office, *Designing Evaluations: 2012 Revision*, Washington, D.C.: U.S. Government Accountability Office, GAO-12-208G, 2012.

U.S. Government Accountability Office, *Program Evaluation: Strategies to Facilitate Agencies' Use of Evaluation in Program Management and Policy Making*, Washington, D.C.: U.S. Government Accountability Office, GAO-13-570, 2013.

U.S. Government Accountability Office, *Program Evaluation: Annual Agency-Wide Plans Could Enhance Leadership Support for Program Evaluations*, Washington, D.C.: U.S. Government Accountability Office, GAO-17-743, 2017.

U.S. Military Entrance Processing Command, "DoDMERB/USMEPCOM Study: Six Sigma Project," presentation to COL Yearly, USMEPCOM Commander, February 10, 2006.

U.S. Military Entrance Processing Command, "The USMEPCOM Story," undated. As of March 8, 2019:
http://www.mepcom.army.mil/About-Us/The-USMEPCOM-Story/

U.S. Military Entrance Processing Command, "USMEPCOM: RAND Study Team," briefing to the project team during site visit to USMEPCOM Headquarters, North Chicago, Ill., August 16, 2016.

U.S. Military Entrance Processing Command Regulation 40-1, "Medical Services Medical Qualification Program," North Chicago, Ill.: U.S. Military Entrance Processing Command, May 23, 2018. As of August 30, 2018:
http://www.mepcom.army.mil/Portals/112/Documents/PubsForms/Regs/r-0040 -001.pdf

U.S. Military Entrance Processing Command Regulation 601-23, "Personnel Procurement Enlistment Processing," North Chicago, Ill.: U.S. Military Entrance Processing Command, October 10, 2017. As of August 30, 2018:
http://www.mepcom.army.mil/Portals/112/Documents/PubsForms/Regs/r-0601 -023.pdf

U.S. Military Entrance Processing Command Regulation 680-3, "United States Military Entrance Processing Command Integrated Resource System (USMIRS)," North Chicago, Ill.: U.S. Military Entrance Processing Command, May 2, 2006. As of August 30, 2018:
http://www.mepcom.army.mil/Portals/112/Documents/PubsForms/Regs/r-0680 -003.pdf

USMEPCOM—*See* U.S. Military Entrance Processing Command.

W. K. Kellogg Foundation, *Logic Model Development Guide*, Battle Creek, Mich., 2004. As of September 25, 2018:
https://www.bttop.org/sites/default/files/public/W.K.%20Kellogg%20LogicModel .pdf